THE MAGIC

OF

QUANTUM LIVING

The Oneness Principle

EDWIN NEL

BALBOA.
PRESS

A DIVISION OF HAY HOUSE

Balboa Press books may be ordered through booksellers or by contacting:

Balboa Press
A Division of Hay House
1663 Liberty Drive
Bloomington, IN 47403
www.balboapress.com
1 (877) 407-4847

Because of the dynamic nature of the Internet, any web addresses or links contained in this book may have changed since publication and may no longer be valid. The views expressed in this work are solely those of the author and do not necessarily reflect the views of the publisher, and the publisher hereby disclaims any responsibility for them.

The author of this book does not dispense medical advice or prescribe the use of any technique as a form of treatment for physical, emotional, or medical problems without the advice of a physician, either directly or indirectly. The intent of the author is only to offer information of a general nature to help you in your quest for emotional and spiritual well-being. In the event you use any of the information in this book for yourself, which is your constitutional right, the author and the publisher assume no responsibility for your actions.

Printed in the United States of America.

ISBN: 978-1-4525-1695-0 (sc)
ISBN: 978-1-4525-1697-4 (hc)
ISBN: 978-1-4525-1696-7 (e)

Library of Congress Control Number: 2014910926

Balboa Press rev. date: 08/05/2014

CONTENTS

ACKNOWLEDGEMENTS

I WOULD LIKE TO EXPRESS my sincere thanks towards my parents, Denver and Serietta Nel, for always being so loving and giving of themselves, forever caring and being there no matter what the occasion or circumstance; you truly excelled at raising my three siblings and I. I love you dearly!

A heartfelt thank you goes out to all my spiritual teachers, but in particular to Charlotte Spirydonova and the group of souls with whom I have spent numerous hours and days over a number of years; working with tremendous vigour, dedicated and focused at shifting old paradigms of beliefs, behaviours and views.

And to my supporters, Celeste van Aswegen and Helena Austen, for taking your time, reading the manuscript and providing me with much needed commentary and feedback; thank you very much.

Lastly, to Nadine Rossouw as my main editor and friend, for your enthusiasm and belief in the final product; immense gratitude and love for helping me make this book my magical reality.

FOREWORD

I AM SO FORTUNATE THAT my journey through life has taught me many life lessons. Only through my experiences and relationships have I been able to write this book with the guidance from spirit. Thank you to my soul, to God and to each and every person whom I have encountered along my journey to date.

I am extremely grateful for every opportunity that enabled me to connect with so many brothers and sisters of the divine human family over the course of my life and to have shared countless intimate moments. Some of these moments and encounters have pushed the boundaries of my belief system to the max. Over time I had to redefine the way I look at my relatedness to my fellow humans, our planet and all experiences; as previously they were viewed through the half-closed eyes and from the limited perspective of a human being raised with strong Christian values, morals and beliefs.

My real awakening started in 2007 when I wanted to save the world from the pain, anguish and suffering; as there was a burning desire emanating from deep within my heart and soul. About a year later I realized that I cannot save anyone let alone the world. It dawned upon me that I only have to save myself, love myself more, each day, and show the way by being loving and giving of myself.

Over the past few years I have worked extremely hard, focused and driven by passion, determination and dedication to change my mind-set about all events, experiences and relationships - both past and present. It is an ongoing process throughout life - being aware of my every thought, word and action in every moment of everyday, always being aware of what I am attracting and creating in life.

I had to endure many obstacles and barriers to date, and know there are still more to be conquered as I venture towards a greater understanding of life, built on a foundation of truth and love.

I had a front row seat and saw many corpses, humans killing other humans whilst spending time in the South African National Defence Force back in 1993, a year before our first independent and free election. I have projected immense hatred and anger towards other human beings - at times even towards my own family members - which I can only ascribe to my limited views and understanding at the time. I have lied. I have cheated and have been cheated on. I have broken promises and trust. I have used people. I have injured many people. I am no saint! I am a normal person like you.

I have parachuted out of airplanes as an airborne soldier. I have hiked up mountains, played rugby, run races and marathons, competed in triathlons and Ironman events, swam, bathed, paddled, canoed, driven, cycled and motorcycled in and across a variety of land areas, seas, rivers and lakes; in, on and around different countries and continents, from South Africa, Lesotho, Zambia, The United States of America, Canada, United Kingdom, France, Monaco, Egypt, Turkey, Nepal, India to Malawi. I have also had to surrender to and have been close to death a few times during my life.

In hindsight, it is my truth that most of these obstacles and experiences had to happen – they are a part of my destiny and have enabled me to teach the truth about life and love firsthand. Over the years I have been exposed to many teachings and belief systems through a variety of religions, and lately including the real essence of truth about love as taught by the ancient schools of knowledge and wisdom. This is some of the knowledge and wisdom which I have gained and will share with you today.

I am by no means out to convince anyone of my truth. I am only sharing with you what I have learned and for some part still busy integrating. Every religion over the past few thousand years has advocated their respective truths as the one and only truth. However, in the process, I believe we have been led like sheep into the lion's den, over and over – countless times, to be slaughtered and for what? To defend our righteous and belief in our God.

Truth and love require nothing, seek nothing, and do not have to prove anything, or be proven, and need not be recognized or validated. It simply **Is**. Every person has a different truth; even sects within organized religion have different beliefs and views. Truth differs according to your mind-set of beliefs, values and views. I challenge you to dig deep, unravel and discover your own truth based on a more expansive love! Go now and find that divine spark of light hidden deep within your own being and recognize that same spark within all of creation above, below, in and around!

INTRODUCTION TO QUANTUM LIVING

WHAT DOES 'QUANTUM LIVING' MEAN for you and I?

The connection of all things and people; everything is connected in the entire universe. Nothing is outside of this scope as all form part of God. Yes, God is everything that ever has been, is and will be. This is the plain and simple reality of quantum physics.

I guess you, I and all of us, want to know more about the dynamics and workings of 'quantum living'. We want to know more about this thing called 'life' and 'existence'. The word *'quantum'*[1] is being used all the time by so many new age and spiritual people around the world. Even scientists are using the word frequently and still trying to figure out and understand the true concept behind the word. They desperately want to know how this concept titled 'quantum physics' or 'quantum mechanics' works.

Scientists have created experiments which transport an atom or a subatomic particle, such as a photon, over vast distances.[2] It has also been proven that both photons and electrons can be at two places at the same time, as these particles are in a quantum

---

[1] Quantum: http://en.wikipedia.org/wiki/Quantum

[2] Quantum teleportation: http://en.wikipedia.org/wiki/Quantum_teleportation

state.[3] This and similar experiments are driving the science fraternity mad as they are frantically trying to understand the rules governing the world of atoms and particles, as all matter is made from energy[4]. How can a particle appear at two places at the same time? It's impossible! Yet science has proven this phenomenon to be true. Why, then, are we as humans not able to do the same? What does quantum living mean for us as humans and people living in the 'real' world? How can we make use of the quantum element?

Where and how do we start to harness the quantum power by living a life filled with inspiration and intuitive synchronicity - this should be the question. In writing this I am channelling the information from my mind which is connected to the other side of the veil - the spirit and God side - for those who do not understand.

God is not one dimensional and linear; God is multi-faceted, multi-dimensional and consists of various aspects, elements and parts. God makes up the universe, all parts - living, and in spirit. The whole aim of God is to know God better, and each one of us is a part of God, or as I would call it, 'we all form a part of God's beautiful tapestry!'

I was listening to a Kryon[5] channelling - a message about intuition and synchronicity this morning, and realized that I know this component well and have been using it to my best ability over the past few years. I have been guided by intuition and synchronicity my whole life; however, I have become much more aware of this very element since the start of my

---

[3]   Double-slit experiment: http://en.wikipedia.org/wiki/Double-slit_experiment

[4]   Energy: http://en.wikipedia.org/wiki/Energy

[5]   Kryon is a loving angelic entity channelled by Lee Carroll. Also referred to as an electromagnetic entity of light. Website: http://www.kryon.com/

spiritual journey. Prior to this awareness, I would interpret these events as random occurrences or just lucky coincidences, not making any real sense.

My journey has been one of great and wonderful experiences leading me to this point in time where I am sitting on a farm in Magaliesburg, South Africa, compiling this manuscript – a small book to assist people with questions about everyday life; thus enabling you to start looking for and expecting the extraordinary. Thoughts of inspiration are flowing as I am writing these words, and it feels amazing to be so connected and able to be channelling this brief. My fingers can hardly keep up with typing and with what I want to say!

As I am typing I am debating whether I should be writing instead of typing the information down. Well there is no wrong or right to this question I am posing to myself. Writing means that all the information will be on paper and I will have to transfer it to my computer later, whereas on the other hand all the information will already be in electronic format, making life easier. This thought causes me to have a little smile as I ponder on the idea.

It's good to laugh at oneself, and not done often enough by most people, nor is having fun, being spontaneous and enjoying the moment. The now! We are forever looking at the next moment and planning ahead instead of taking pleasure in the present. Herein lies the magic of understanding the quantum theory of life: 'stay present and enjoy the moment' – the past does not exist, the future also does not exist; only the now exists and this is where we should ideally be living life.

However, too often we look to the future and miss the present; we miss the opportunities and magic the present moment has to offer. Stop right there and look around and see what you are doing! Stop planning and start living in the now!

God has always existed and will always exist. That is a constant and it does not matter who you are speaking to – most people in the world believe in a higher power and afterlife. Our intuitive inborn human programming is to believe in God.

Exercise 1 – Contemplate God

Before we continue I want you to spend a few moments in deep contemplation of three questions:

- Who is God?
- What is God?
- Where is God?

Close and place the book next to you. Have your journal ready whilst sitting quietly and contemplating these three questions, writing down your initial thoughts and ideas on these concepts. Let your realization be your guide and allow love and inspiration to find you along the path in guiding you towards your answers.

ANCIENT QUESTIONS ABOUT UNDERSTANDING THE HUMAN PUZZLE AND GOD

NOW THERE I LOST MY chain of thought...God is forever and will forever be! So why are we on the earth? What are we doing here on the earth? Thoughts of 'life is so difficult I cannot go on', 'I am tired', 'I am lost', 'I am scared and do not know what to do next' vibrate through our minds. These and many more questions are being asked by scores of people all around the world, all with the purpose and wish to better understand the meaning of life.

My simple response is that you are here to discover, and make known the unknown. If you knew everything and how your life would unfold, would you enjoy each moment? The answer is a strong, 'of course not'. How could you if you already know the ending?

Immediately, without delay, as if to testify and amplify the above declaration, there was a sharp influx of heat and energy in my physical body. I can feel God's divine love and compassion filling my being, my every atom and cell. I want to cry from the joy and happiness of just being alive and able to channel this piece of much needed information from the other side of the veil. I am listening, and you can send the inspirational messages. Thank you my Friend, my Brother, my Sister; I honour and love You always.

We are born into forgetfulness with the purpose of exploring and experiencing life and all it has to offer. I concede that it can be very difficult at times, as there are bad things that happen to each one of us. Allow me to rephrase the statement by saying that there are so-called 'bad things' that 'happen to us'. However, it is all a matter of perspective. These are not really 'bad things' which are happening to you; all this is just part of the whole experience of being human. You are here to grow and change; evolving until you wholly realize your divinity as being God.

Yes, you heard right; the main purpose of the journey of life is to remember who you are. To remember that you are part, a piece of God. The puzzle is to navigate through this life or maybe the next or even the life after that until you finally realize you are God, and without a shadow of a doubt know this truth. We are all family. You may have brothers, sisters or parents who are your biological family; however each and every person on the planet is also your family. I have to make this point very clear. **Every person** on the planet is part of God's great tapestry.

The Bible refers to 'Christ's body'.[6] However, it is my truth that it should be interpreted as, 'God's body'. What I mean is that we are all a part of God's body, and we are here on Earth to lend a hand in each person's experience of discovering his or her greatness and magnificence. At times it can be gruelling and harsh as we experience difficult and arduous times in our lives. These experiences push the boundaries of our human mind's programming and belief patterns. The difficult or tough experiences, as they are labelled, all form part of the process of life, helping us grow by becoming wiser day by day.

---

[6] New American Standard Bible, New Testament in the book of 1 Corinthians 12:27.

Some people may say that we are in the school called 'life'. We are learning to evolve and should be enjoying the process and journey of life. The existence of horrible and dreadful incidents for example, being raped, shot or murdered are being questioned by many. I believe that most of the time the events in our lives are planned by divine timing and are meant to happen. Yes, even the 'bad things', form part of the quantum system.

The school of life does not only have 'bad things', but also has a multitude of 'good things' happening all around the world. For example, we are cultivating and becoming more loving than ever before, we are gradually building new respect for our planet and the sacredness earth holds for all life. We are slowly viewing all human life as holy and more compassion is being displayed in times of need and despair. We are evolving for the good of the entire human race.

GOD AND THE WHOLE UNIVERSE IS MADE FROM ENERGY AND PARTICLES

THE QUANTUM SYSTEM IS BEAUTIFUL and there is a reason for everything that comes into existence. God knows everything and you believe this truth, don't you? I know that most people believe that God knows everything and many people will state that Satan is running around and responsible for the injustices of the world, killing people and causing so much pain and destruction on our planet. This is not the case. In fact, it is humans who are doing the so called 'bad and evil things' to other humans.

Each and every human has a part to play on the planet and where the earth is headed. Yes, we all do, and this can be tough at times as we move along the journey of life. We hit stumbling blocks and face harsh and difficult realities and at times have no idea where we are headed. We make mistakes as we grow, but actually, we are learning along the way as there is no such thing as mistakes.

Just know all experiences form part of life's journey, and whether you label it as 'good or bad', it is just an experience that your soul has asked to have in order to catapult it into the next frequency and vibratory level. Energy is made up of atoms and particles which is the source of the universe and all of existence.[7] In Genesis, the Bible refers to the fact that God created man in His own image.[8] You are the universe and inside of you is God. God, the God that you are, has asked to have and learn certain life lessons along your path, moving towards a higher and grander understanding of yourself. We are learning, growing and experiencing as our journey through life unfolds.

Everything is energy and energy can be transformed into higher or lower levels, if it so wishes.[9] In order for us to transform and evolve we need to experience life and accept a greater part of who we are, namely, that we are made up of energy.

Scientists have discovered that some particles, such as protons and neutrons, have mass, whereas photons have no mass. The Higgs boson or 'God particle' is believed to be the particle that gives matter mass.[10] Science is still underway to prove and define this phenomenon as they have not fully verified the workings and relationship between the 'God particle' and others.

Whether you believe it or not, the universe is an intelligent design system. If you disagree, just look around and see for yourself the workings of the world and all systems functioning in relation with each other; from the smallest systems like that of bacterial life to the larger systems like those of the plant, animal and human kingdoms. The presence of God can be seen in all things – all things are interlinked, and as a result, at some level, is a part of God.

---

[7]   Universe: http://en.wikipedia.org/wiki/Universe
[8]   New American Standard Bible, Old Testament in the book of Genesis 1:27.
[9]   Energy transformation: http://en.wikipedia.org/wiki/Energy_transformation
[10]   Higgs boson: http://en.wikipedia.org/wiki/Higgs_boson

TIME AND SPACE IS THE FOUNDATION TO EXPERIENCE LIFE

IMAGINE FOR A SECOND THAT there was no time and space. Do you think you would be able to experience life as we know it? The easy answer is 'no'. We cannot experience anything without time and space. Time and space was created with the specific reason to enable us to experience – it is for this very reason we, as Gods, have come down from the heavens (if that is your truth) to experience life in the physical.

However, time and space as we currently know it creates a false sense of separation between people, places, things and events in our lives. We perceive ourselves as disconnected from other people and elements of life. The paradox is that we need other people, places, times and events in our lives in order to create, experience and take pleasure in, or benefit from as we venture through life.

As previously stated, every person is a part of God, and as such is God – God cannot be separated. Therefore, each person as part of God and God themselves has a unique destiny which is unfolding as they create, explore and grow along the way. Your journey is not the same as your neighbour's journey, or that of your biological sister or brother. We are helping each other to grow in order to experience, in my view, higher parts and planes of life and existence. Our ultimate mission: **'To love ourselves and all life with grace and compassion!'**

The challenging part is being able to understand that there are no wrongs and rights; there are only experiences to be had by the person whilst progressing and walking through life. I have spoken at length that all of life is just about experiences, and you probably want to know more about what this thing called 'quantum' means for you.

We are learning to love and be more accepting of each other. Experiences and relationships are the prime catalysts for learning to love all of life more. Experiences and all relationships are the two keys in life; assisting us with becoming a fully realized God as the Masters have done on our planet, and others, like the Pleiades, Orion and those before them. By the term 'Master' I refer to the term 'God-man' realized in the example of Jesus, Buddha, Krishna, Elijah, Ramtha, Muhammad and many more prophets. They all realized their divinity as a man being a God.

The journey is a never ending story and the story can be difficult at times, with many lessons and hardships along the way. It is my truth that the planet is past the worst part, and we are heading into 'the golden age era' as many ancient and spiritual teachings have described it.

However, before we reach the golden age era, there will still be some complex and uneasy times ahead of us as the old ways of thinking linked to negative and dark energy are going to die hard. It takes time to shift into a new paradigm of living, with more compassion and love for each human and all parts of our planet, whether it be the bacterial, plant, animal or human kingdoms. All forms of life have an important contribution towards creating an environment where we can prosper and experience the enjoyment of living life in its purest form.

Life is precious and most people take it for granted and live a selfish life just thinking of themselves. And oh boy, I can relate as I have done so on many occasions, just thinking about myself and not about the hurt caused to others by my thoughts, words and actions. We are creatures of habit and old habits die hard. The old behaviours and energy want to stay and take you out of the present moment, thus paralyzing you from seeing events for what they truly are. It all forms part of the old energy system; a system where most people are completely unconscious of their selfish thoughts, words and actions.

Old energy and habits are difficult to break; as they are the beliefs and patterns we have built up over a lifetime. Years of reinforced brainwave activity makes it almost impossible to change and let go of our old thinking habits. Breaking these old habits form a vital part of life's journey; to see with new eyes, to hear with new ears and to listen with a new awareness. Intuition is our new compass; start listening to your next intuitive thought of what to do, create or where to go. Intuition is our inborn guidance system, there to help us navigate towards a better and brighter life. All we have to do is tune in and listen to our God.

Exercise 2 – Negative habits

Contemplate on the negative habits which are not supporting your development towards a grander life. Start with the negative habits that you are consciously aware of, for example; smoking, excessive drinking, little or no physical exercise, an eating disorder, procrastination, etc. Your aim should be to examine and establish any harmful physical habits without judging yourself.

We are working backwards to discover and identify our physical habits, before we proceed to the next stage, namely to identify the cause of the relevant habit.

Write down all the negative habits. Be honest and do not leave any negative habits out of the exercise. Remember you are working with the soul which is based on a premise of total and complete honesty.

The next step is to examine, identify and write down the habits and triggers that cause your smoking, excessive drinking, lack of physical exercise, eating disorder, procrastination, etc. This could be related to emotions; such as low self-esteem, low self-worth, stress, trauma, guilt, shame, fear, rejection, etc. or even parental, peer and societal influences.

Finally, sit quietly and become aware of the thoughts passing through your mind; your mental programming and indoctrination creating these negative habits. All habits, whether 'good or bad' start in the mind and from there they are manifested in your physical reality. Become aware of your mind's judgments, logic, analysis and rationale for your negative habits; for example justifications on being poor, being unsuccessful, being ugly, not being good enough, not being supported, you are going to fail, etc. Your mind is coagulating a belief pattern with your every thought and sending powerful signals of energy into the quantum field.

I want to emphasize that you must never judge yourself! I am simply establishing a foundation for the workings of the brain and 'human mind' by making you consciously aware of your thought process being on auto-pilot. For now your observation and awareness of these negative habits and thinking patterns are all that is required.

THE ONENESS PRINCIPLE - ALL IS GOD

GOD, YOUR GOD, IS CONSTANTLY speaking to you even though you might not be hearing the messages. You might be closed off from receiving the answers or from the way the answers are being broadcasted to you. God uses many ways to speak to us humans. He or She speaks through intuitive thoughts received during meditation or prayer, through signs on billboards, words in songs, messages from friends, family and even people you have never before met. All messages are there to guide you to a higher understanding of who you are.

Understanding is a principle we like to discuss and talk about and even throw around at large. Our need for understanding is great and has to make logical sense in our reality, and when it does not, we discard the theory. Well that is exactly what I am doing now, I am busy writing and I have no inclination of where this is headed or which messages will be channelled through me.

I can further explain this concept; as there is a part of me that wants to know what the outcome of the writing this book will be. This part of my being wants to make sense, know and understand the process of writing before actually having experienced it. However, only through having experiences in life and in this case, (writing the book) can I gain a greater understanding based on knowledge and wisdom. This is very much like learning how to ride a bike, only once you have managed to stay on do you have the knowledge of how to ride and thus have gained the understanding from the experience.

The unknown experienced leads to new knowledge and wisdom which, in turn, leads to understanding and the known.

When it comes to God, the quantum state and how the world and everything therein connects and operates, your current understanding must be set aside. Whether you believe it or not, we are all connected. We breathe the same air, don't we? Then you have to agree that no matter what religion you are or background you have, or in what country you live, the connection remains. We are all family and a part of God.

'Only one God'. These are the words I wrote when I initially opened a Facebook account in response to the question, 'what is your religion?' That was more than a year before my spiritual journey started –*'the quest for truth and love'* – and at the time I had no idea what the words truly meant. But now I can say without a doubt we are all connected and family of the body of God.

The Bible also proclaims that there is only one God; 'There is one body and one Spirit, just as also you were called in one hope of your calling; one Lord, one faith, one baptism, one God and Father of all who is over all and through all and in all'.[11]

Whether what I am writing is true for you or not isn't important. The fact remains, however, that we are all born into the physical world with a forgetfulness of who we are. We are then instilled with a longing and yearning to establish the

---

[11] New American Standard Bible, New Testament in the book of Ephesians 4:4-6.

purpose and journey to remember who we really are. We are all family and are here to support and care for each other along the journey of remembering who we are.

No one is more important than the next person, and no one is higher than the next person. The Masters who walked this planet and are still present today advocate the same message. Love and compassion is what makes the world go around; not money, fame and glory! Masters did not and do not want recognition or praise. They want something much more precious than money or gold – to be united with the core of their being inside. They want to be united with God's love that connects them to all life and enables them to live life with truth.

The 'Christ' lies dormant within each one of us. Yes, inside you is God! God is waiting in anticipation to come out and experience the true meaning of life. A God who wants to come out from hiding and to love without fear or lack, making the most of each moment for what that moment has to offer. A God so bright, the whole world can see your light and feel your presence.

THE PURPOSE BEHIND
ALL EXPERIENCES

SLOWLY, SO VERY SLOWLY WE start to peel away the layers of the onion to get to the core. With the strip of each layer our reality expands and we free ourselves from past judgments, hurts and pains which have closed us from the inside and made us shrivel away from life as we cannot bear the pain and suffering anymore.

Our experiences of suffering start to consume our human minds and being, and as a result of this we start to build walls around our heart. The aching wounds of yet another failed relationship or being rejected by another person cannot be accepted by us as we forget that the main purpose of the journey is to remember who we are, and we can only do this through experience. We think and say to ourselves, 'no, I cannot feel this pain again, it hurts too much! I have to protect my broken heart from being life's battering ram of experiences'.

Allow me to emphasize and explain an important mind shifting principle to you – all experiences are and were the result your choice – you always have a choice on how you perceive an experience. Some people will have a perceived truly 'bad' experience but will pose the questions: 'what can I take away from this?' or 'what should I make of this experience?' These people are wise as they have realized that all 'bad' experiences are just part of learning and they were responsible for attracting the experiences into their lives with the sole purpose to learn, grow and become wiser.

Yes, you heard me right; you have consciously or unconsciously been attracting experiences into your life in order to learn, grow and become wiser than the previous day. Life is a part of everything and as we expand we discover that we mustn't take anything personally. Learning not to take anything personally remains a very difficult life lesson for most of us, but hopefully over time, and with numerous interactions do we finally come to the realization of this truth.

I know there are those people who will go out of their way to make life difficult for others as they always want their own way. They have their own very small view of the world - a view being playing out in their head of how they should act and react to others. This is all a part of the quantum system which I am expanding on in this book.

The word 'quantum' means so much more than we think, and we are still trying to understand and make sense of how it works. The main reason for your being on earth is to learn to be God. A God who can manifest anything your heart desires - this potential is available for you. You just need to accept this fact and so it will be.

I have spoken about this thing called 'quantum', and you, as the reader are undoubtedly curious to get to know more of the workings of this system. It's a highly intelligent system with an ever-changing, infinite scope of possibilities at work to guide you through life. *YOU* are quantum, you just might not be aware of it. You are always connected to and one with God - that which is physical is always connected to that which is spiritual.

The two sides of the veil is in reality only one, but appears as separate in the 'human-mind' where duality exists. Once you let go of the 'human-mind' and merge with the Mind of God separation ceases and oneness transcends through, in and around your being. Again I want to make reference to Ephesians 4: 4-6 in the Bible.[12]

Each person on this planet has a part of their being connected to the physical and to the spiritual sides of the veil – on the spiritual side of the veil, God and all humans as part of God are working to create 'magic' (reality) on the physical side of the veil, through intuitive thought and ideas emanating from God's Mind. See new ideas as intuitive thought originating from God's Mind as your connection to the spiritual side. Each thought has the potential to be manifested into the physical, if pursued with hard work, dedication and belief.

Experiences are being planned and arranged by you and your God connection: either for you to enjoy life or to grow, evolve and come to an understanding of your greatness. You always have a choice how you will proceed in life. There is nobody but yourself telling you what to do and what not to do; you always have your own free will and choice.

In life we are guided by our moral values – the beliefs and views we hold dear in our hearts. If you think it is alright to kill a donkey, a whale or murder another person, then that is your moral code; the belief and view you subscribe to. Now, I am not labelling any as correct or incorrect. You are responsible for the constraints, beliefs and views in your life. Your moral values and consciousness will determine the actions you are willing to take in order to create your reality.

---

[12] New American Standard Bible, New Testament in the book of Ephesians 4:4-6 - **4** *There is* one body and one Spirit, just as also you were called in one hope of your calling; **5** one Lord, one faith, one baptism, **6** one God and Father of all who is over all and through all and in all.

We all have our own subjective reality and we all form part of a greater reality, namely the collective reality or consciousness of the planet. An even greater reality exists, that of the universal consciousness which includes everything seen in the universe. Lastly, there is a consciousness which even includes the unseen elements, and this consciousness is made up of everybody and everything past, present, future, dead or alive; otherwise known as the whole. I call it 'God' or 'Super Consciousness'.

Nothing can live and exist outside of this whole, which is everything that ever was, is and will be. With the 'whole' I endeavour to encapsulate God's creation in its majestic and glorious entirety. Ponder and think about this for a while, not only comprehending the magnitude of this thought but also the minuteness thereof. It is an interesting paradox that exits in time and space, and was created to allow us to live and experience the whole, wholly in the now.

WE ARE THE GODS OF CREATION

MOVING ON TO THE NEXT part of the teaching. We, all of us, created the universe and everything inside the universe – the earth, the sun and the planets all form a part of who we are. There isn't a thing that is **not** a part of who we are, and we are here to remember that everything is connected and everything is 'us' at the same time. An interesting thought to consider and explore.

We, as Gods, came down from the highest invisible light spectrum to experience what we had created. According to science, the universe is estimated to be a whopping 13.8 billion earth years old.[13] We descended to experience the whole universe and planets within, and all life contained within these planets and earth; for instance water, air, fire, animals, plants, trees, fellow humans, etc. We yearned to be a part of our creation to see, taste, touch, smell and hear in the physical sense of the word. So we created a way in order for us to experience our creation and as such gave birth to the human body.

We are Gods that decided to come down from the invisible light spectrum by reducing our energy, our frequency and vibration for the purpose of entering the physical plane in order to experience our creation. Involution was born as we descended and came to live on earth as humans. Earth is not

---

[13] Age of the universe: http://en.wikipedia.org/wiki/Age_of_the_universe

the first or only planet with life in the universe; there are other planets that have gone through similar advances. The possibility could even exist that you may once have lived on another planet.

In the Bible there are various references to all people being 'gods'.[14] We are all Gods, but we do not know this fact to be true. Since the journey is about remembering who we are, it is about navigating our way back to the Source or God by making known the unknown. Some of what I have covered in this book has been written in much more detail by others; these concepts and teachings will therefore be familiar to some. Still more needs to be introduced with regards to the above concepts before we can progress to the next level of this teaching. We need to discuss the dynamics of quantum physics, how it all fits into being human and how we can use the aspects to work for us in everyday life.

As Gods, we descended unto the Earth plane as it is called. We lowered our energy by lowering our frequency and vibration in order to make this happen. Reference to this fact can be found in the New American Standard Bible where Jacob was given a vision from God, see Genesis 28 verse 12; 'He had a dream, and behold, a ladder was set on the earth with its top reaching to heaven; and behold, the angels of God were ascending and descending on it'.

---

[14] New American Standard Bible, Old Testament in the book of Psalm 82:6 – I said, 'You are gods, And all of you are sons of the Most High.' and in the New Testament in the book of John 10:34 – Jesus answered them, 'Has it not been written in your Law, 'I SAID, YOU ARE GODS '?'.

Everything is energy – a known and proven fact by most people on the planet. Science has confirmed that energy never dies, it only transforms into higher or lower states of existence.[15]

Okay, so everything is energy and energy never dies; now what? Energy transforms and this principle can easily be seen with the physical eye through, for example, water turning into ice or steam. Water in its liquid form turns into ice when frozen; changing back into liquid when heated, and when heated even further, water turns into steam and evaporates into the air.

Food offers another example of energy transformation. Food contains vital energy in the form of carbohydrates, fats and proteins, essential for all humans to live. We ingest food into our bodies whereby our body's digestive system transforms the food into energy much needed for our daily survival.

These are two examples to explain the principle of energy transformation. Ask any scientist for more and you will be met with an excited response and numerous examples illustrating the principle of energy transformation.

We are learning to love and be Gods of creation, by making known the unknown. If you knew everything there is to know, what would then be the purpose of living? To do the same thing day in and day out, like the movie 'Ground Hog Day'? How boring and frustrating would life be if this was the case, with everything staying the same and no new experiences to be had. Part of the journey of the soul is to explore all dimensions of life; acquiring valuable wisdom from knowledge gathered throughout life's journey and its many experiences.

---

[15] Energy transformation: http://en.wikipedia.org/wiki/Energy_transformation

JOY COMES FROM
LIVING IN THE NOW

SEE HOW YOUR LIFE CHANGES by simply waking up each day with the consciousness that this is your first and last day, your only day alive and to go about in that fashion. Nothing in life is cast in stone – just look at the tsunamis, earthquakes, hurricanes and other natural disasters around the world. We must all be happy and enjoy each day for what that day has to offer. We must be open to receive the blessings and gifts available, whilst smiling as we live each moment in the now.

We must stop thinking of the next day and the day after that, and start living in the here and now wherever we are. This is the only time that counts, the present second, and once it has gone, we must let it go; the past is the past and we should always aim to stay in the now. Live for each second and what that second may bring. Live each second with your whole being to the fullest of your ability, as in that second lies the joy and the exhilaration of life, the bliss and nirvana the Masters know and have spoken about.

Masters live life only in the now and never think about the past – they therefore create their future from the now (as opposed from the past, which most people in the world do). Masters are living each moment in the now and with that comes a joy mostly unknown to this plane. Most of us can but dream of such an amazing experience. It's not just an experience, it's a state of mind that you enter into by way of your thinking, it's yours for the taking at any time you so desire.

To access this state of mind, all you have to do is change your thinking, because everything is mind, created from the individual's viewpoint and perspective. Joy is a state of mind, peace is a state of mind, happiness is a state of mind, depression is a state of mind, lack is a state of mind, anger is a state of mind; and so on. Your mind is your greatest tool on this journey called life and you have the power over your attitude and over the way you see and think about anything in life.

THE QUANTUM THEORY OF ENERGY AND CREATING EXPERIENCES

YOU CAN THINK OF AN experience as good or bad – this is entirely your choice and point of view. Some people will say a robbery was bad and others will say it was a good thing. The way the robbery could be viewed as a 'good thing' is because it may have made those being robbed more aware to stay focused and alert in the present moment. A big part of our journey is to be present with whatever you are doing and to take pleasure in the moment for what the moment has to offer.

You are the creator, whether consciously or unconsciously, somewhere along the way the robbery was planned by you for you. The robbery was meant to happen to sharpen your sword and make you more attentive and present in the moment. I am not judging the robbery as 'good or bad'; I am merely saying it gifted you with much needed focus and presence.

Maybe the robbery or something else which you experienced was unpleasant; however you are the one responsible for drawing the experience into your reality, whether you consciously think so or not. This is the model and workings of all experiences in the quantum field and system. Whether you agree or not, everything is quantum and has a quantum part to play.

Everything is energy, as energy is the basic building blocks of all life. Even the seemingly open spaces of air are filled with particles of quantum energy waiting to be used or transformed. Thus all particles of energy are forever quantumly connected; and they are continuously being altered and rearranged in order to create a new experience for you.

How do you think Jesus was able to walk on the water,[16] or Moses was able to perform all the miracles we read in the Bible?[17] Energy has the ability to transform and forms part of the quantum principle that applies to everything that is life. We have a part of our being on the physical side of the veil, but most of who we are is in fact sitting on the other side of the veil. The truth is that there is no real separation between the two sides. They are interlinked, but we just can't see the other side with our physical eyes as yet.

---

[16] New American Standard Bible, New Testament in the book on Matthew 14: 22 – 33, and Mark 6: 45 – 52, and John 6: 16 – 21.

[17] New American Standard Bible, Old Testament all throughout the book of Exodus.

THE ETERNAL PROGRESSION
OF THE SOUL

ONE OF THE PURPOSES OF the journey for all souls is to remember that we are far greater than our physical bodies. Our body is our vehicle which we have become so accustomed to over the course of our lives. We are not the physical body; we are far larger than our bodies. I know this message so well and have been reminded by so many people of this very fact over the span of my life and by now the terminology in second nature to me.

We think in terms of our physical body, but in actual fact this is a very small portion of who in truth we are. We are huge, amazing and magnificent divine beings of light. Words fall short and can barely describe our sheer beauty and greatness.

Experiences are created by us for us to lead us towards higher realization of who we are. These experiences are brought to us by our spirit and God with the aim and sole reason to grow and evolve – this is the main journey of the soul – to experience the full glorification of being a living and breathing God in all our magnificence. I know the same has been said by me and other people before, but for me it's important that those who are reading and hearing these written words for the first time will find truth and recognition in them.

Each person has a unique life path and chose their body in order to have the experiences necessary for them to grow and evolve. This is an intricate concept to acknowledge, but some religions like the Hindus, Kabbalah followers, a sect within Judaism and even sects within Christianity and Islam have believers in reincarnation. Our souls are eternally progressing; the soul is your and my core, directly connected and one with God's love. Life after life, we come back to venture into the unknown, exploring aspects of ourselves.

The soul draws experiences to itself with the purpose to learn, grow and evolve into a greater being. Did you realize I said 'itself'? This is because the soul is not male or female. God cannot be divided into gender. God is everything and has no boundaries! We are all that, we have no boundaries and are a part of everything. This is a concept that I am personally still busy with fully integrating and understanding.

With each experience we are growing, and as we grow, so does our light grow within us; our light energy transforming into higher spectrums. The more light we hold the higher is our vibration and frequency. In the Bible Jesus said, 'I am the light of the world'.[18] With these words he proclaims that he has realized the light is within him. We can all do the same and free our light to shine, as we learn from life's experiences. How else will we grow?

There is another verse in the Bible declaring, 'When I was a child, I used to speak like a child, think like a child, reason like a child; when I became a man, I did away with childish things'.[19] This verse refers to growth as we journey through life's many lessons until finally being able to see and know as God does. The Masters came to teach us of unconditional love and compassion for each other, yet many people for centuries

---

[18] New American Standard Bible, New Testament in the book of John 8: 12.
[19] New American Standard Bible, New Testament in the book of 1 Corinthians 13:11.

and millennia have made war to defend their belief and point of view.

There is an old proverb declaring the following: 'If women ruled the world, they would never send their sons to do battle'. Most women have a deeper understanding of the sacredness of life. They feel and see life grow inside them; they know the true meaning behind the words 'unconditional love' and 'compassion'. How can they sacrifice any of their children to die in battle?

Those of you who are parents, mothers and fathers; do you love any of your kids differently or do you have the same love and affection for each one? God loves all children the same and draws no divide between any – this is pure unconditional love. A God who does not love all His or Her children equally is not a God of mine, because how can one child be more important than another? I believe in a loving God, a God with no restrictions on His or Her love, a love which transcends human barriers and comprehension, a love so remarkable and wonderfully perfect.

We all come from the same place with blood flowing through our veins – how else could we be here? Why are we, then, so different in our view of God and what He or She wants for our lives? We have forgotten our divinity that we are all Gods and we are the ones creating everything in our life by our every thought, word and deed. We are creating everyday and all day by our mere thoughts as they carry the Creator's energy with them.

Exercise 3 - Thoughts

Place the book down, and sit quietly for a few moments becoming aware of each and every thought passing through your mind. Do not judge any of your thoughts; just be the observer of your mind, by consciously becoming aware of each and every thought being projected into the quantum field. Thoughts of lack, abundance, self-doubt, self-belief, self-respect, self-worth, self-image, self-love, self-rejection, self-importance, humility, guilt, innocence, unhappiness, joy, self-sabotage, jealousy, trust, anger, irritation, calmness, resentment, kindness, and many more thoughts which are just happening and later being manifested for you.

As with exercise two, I want you to become aware of your human mind's programming being on auto-pilot; feeling as if you do not have any control over your mind. You are not the **'human thinking mind'**! Nevertheless, you have become so accustomed to a pattern and program of thinking since your birth, which we are going to break down, little by little. Only by way of observation and awareness can we start to change old negative thinking patterns, beliefs and views that do not serve our highest good and potential.

OUR THINKING CREATES OUR REALITY - 'GOOD OR BAD'

MONITORING OUR THOUGHTS IS CRUCIAL as we are projecting into the quantum field with our every thought. We are constantly formulating pictures of what we want from life and of how we see the world. The interesting truth remains that most people still do not even know how important monitoring their every thought is. Our every thought has creative power in the quantum field. We are carving our reality out by the very way we think and that is a proven truth.

In the Old Testament we find the following Bible verse, 'For as he thinks within himself, so he is'.[20] These very important and wise words should be taken to mind and heart by all humans. The primary reason why we should start with changing our thinking is because, ultimately when we do, we also start changing our view of love. As we open up towards a more expansive love, our reality and world starts to change. Start seeing the impact that your every thought has on the whole and observe that when we project negative energy onto others, we open up for negativity to be projected back onto us too.

Start with self-examination by changing the way you think and feel about others and every event and all experiences you

---

[20] New Standard American Bible, Old Testament in the book of Proverbs 23:7.

have had in your life to date. Every event was finely planned and orchestrated in order for you to develop and have an experience. By your thinking you are attracting events and situations into your life, from lack to abundance.

If you only think good things and let go of the bad you will mostly experience only joy with unsurpassed happiness. However when something bad does happen you should ask the questions, 'what can I learn from this event?' and 'how did I create this scenario?' By doing so you have not tied into the reaction of lashing out at someone or the event, you merely accepted it as necessary in order to learn and grow.

You have not allowed yourself to suffer and thus your energy is freer than before. You have gained more knowledge and wisdom by increasing your awareness and consciousness, and in doing so your frequency and vibration is higher. New experiences in life have the potential to bring with them a change in thinking, beliefs and views. Freedom from suffering is the main goal and can only be attained by thinking differently – the choice is always yours.

So many of us are defined by a bad experience and we struggle to cope and move forward in life. As a result we push back and hide away, scared to live due to the pain and suffering we felt from losing a loved one or having had a bad experience like being raped or molested. Know that even these experiences form part of a greater picture that I am busy painting for you. These truths are harsh realities which are extremely difficult to grasp and understand for our human minds.

GOD NEVER JUDGES,
NEVER HAS NEVER WILL

Even this is part of the quantum potentials existing in the field of possibilities and ingrained into a world where the reality of duality exists. I may have lost some of you here, and I need to make myself clear. These principles are not easy to understand for our human minds. The above has to do with the workings of your reality within a larger reality, and both realities have an infinite number of potentials that simultaneously exist.

We are learning the basic workings of life and all of existence, a quantum system of energy and consciousness creating the interconnectedness between the physical and spiritual sides of the veil. The main principle of God is to make known the unknown, and in order for this to occur we need time, space and an event to take place in the now. This creates a merging of two or more realities creating an experience.

Before I continue with my next point I want to emphasize that God is everything, whether you label it as good or bad. Nothing is **not** God, and God consists of and is everything on both the physical and spiritual sides of the veil. Nothing falls outside of God or Source. For those preferring, I use the word 'Source' to describe the great and magnificent Omnipresent, Omniscient and Omnipotent God whom encompasses everything known and unknown.

Another important principle is that God or Source is not human and does not judge, never has and never will. 'It' is incapable of doing so and only has love and compassion for everyone and everything, because it is everyone and everything.

Exercise 4 - Judgment

It is my view that the following exercise is not only the most difficult, but also the most important exercise that you will ever embark on. The aim is purifying the thinking of your human mind. Once again, without judging yourself, contemplate any and all judgments that you hold of yourself and any person with regards to race, physical appearance, intellect, emotional state, mental state, personality, attitude, wealth, lack of wealth, success, lack of success, etc. You will immediately know what yardsticks are for you.

Next, write down all things you are judging in the world. Remember, awareness is the key to setting yourself free. You may have judgments that relate to current world and local governmental, economic, financial and monetary policies; for example health reform policies, same sex relationships and marriages, etc. You are entitled to your opinion and view, but never judge anything.

> *'Love is the observation without judgment!'*
> *- Dalai Lama, Ramtha and others*

Have an opinion, but do not send more negative and dark energy into the world by judging anything. Judgment is like looking into a mirror and the reflections of light are being cast straight back at you. Be the eternal observer of your mind and without judgment, allow every person to be who they want to be.

The next step is to slowly let go of your judgments and projections. Our brains have been created to judge, and most of these judgments and projections stem from parental, peer and societal influences and are based upon a belief or view. Sit quietly and contemplate each judgment, by turning inwards and asking your God for assistance in the process. Ask yourself, 'why have I been judging that person or thing?', 'is this my truth or just a belief and view which has been imposed upon me?' Let the love of God guide you towards the answers of the truth. Remember, true love never judges, true love is like falling in love with that someone special where you only see their good qualities!

The last step is for you to make this new found truth a knowingness, by living it daily. Please, do not be hard on yourself, as this exercise may take a lifetime or more to perfect. Just know that with every judgmental thought, negative energy is being placed, directed and sent into the quantum field. At some point in time you will have to face each and every ripple that you created, the wave of energy has to make its way back to you. Know that with every judgment you shift, there is more freedom that enters your mind.

'Learn how to see, realize that everything connects
to everything else.' - Leonardo da Vinci

THE REALITY OF DUALITY

ENERGY IS DRAWN TOGETHER FOR the purpose to create and have an experience. See it as a positive and a negative magnet being drawn to connect, and no matter how hard the positive or negative magnet tries to repudiate, the force keeps on pulling them together. The closer they come into orbit with the other, the more difficult it gets to stay apart, and eventually the two poles collide, bumping heads.

Our universe and all matter are made from energy and appear as duality. We live in a reality of duality and this is the primary reason how we can experience life on earth. Allow me to explain. If there was only light, how would you know darkness? If there was only hot, how would you know cold? If there was only short, how would you know tall? If there is no money, how would you distinguish wealth and riches from that of poverty or lack? If there was no sickness, how would you know health and wellness? There exists an opposite for everything in life; we are born into a world of duality.

This is called the force of 'good and evil'[21] where the Bible and Torah introduce us to the principle of 'sin' in the book of Genesis. The Bible, however, has a different meaning and

---

[21] New American Standard Bible, Old Testament in the book of Genesis 3:22 - Then the LORD God said, 'Behold, the man has become like one of Us, knowing good and evil; and now, he might stretch out his hand, and take also from the tree of life, and eat, and live forever'.

interpretation to that of the Jewish Torah. In the Christian Bible the 'evil force' is said be caused by Lucifer or Satan, one of God's fallen angels; and repenting your sins are the key to be saved by Jesus, the only son of God for the purpose of attaining eternal life and entering the kingdom of heaven upon your death.

On the other hand, in the Jewish Torah, 'Satan' is merely an idiom or parable and refers more to the 'knowledge from the tree of life'.[22] Judaism holds the view that all people sin at various points in their lives, as the human mind has a tendency to evil. Therefore God in His mercy allowed people to repent and be forgiven.

The Quran in the Islamic religion applies a similar principle to the Christian and Jewish faiths, where the act of sin goes against Allah or God, bringing punishment to the individual on the Day of Judgment.

Buddhism, on the other hand, refers to the two opposing principles of good and evil as not a reality and must be emptied or overcome to achieve oneness. From all main spiritual teachings, the Buddhist interpretation of these forces is as close to an absolute truth as we will find about life.

God introduced the principle of duality in order for all souls to experience, learn, grow and find their way back to the light and God. We do this by making known the unknown. We are endeavouring to know and see each person as God. As the Eastern and Asian Nations around India would say, 'Namaste', meaning, 'I see and greet the God in you'. Profound words of wisdom bearing ancient knowledge that all humans are made in the image of God and divine. God is inside each one of us, and it is for us to discover this truth by switching on our light.

---

[22] Old Testament in the book of Genesis 3:22 – Then the LORD God said, 'Behold, the man has become like one of Us, knowing good and evil; and now, he might stretch out his hand, and take also from the tree of life, and eat, and live forever'.

EVALUATING AND COMPARING FORM A PART OF THE REALITY OF DUALITY

DUALITY IS VITAL FOR EXPERIENCING life, as we measure and compare everything with our physical eyes. We think to ourselves, 'should I have my eggs scrambled, fried or poached?', 'should I be more like him or her?', or, 'what new car should I buy?' We are consistently comparing everything we see, do and want whether we are buying toothpaste or buying a home. We look at the brand, we look at the price and compare what would be best for us and at the same time suit our pockets. It's a system of duality, comparing and analyzing high and low prices to quality and durability. We are navigating duality the best way we know in order to survive and prosper.

We buy products, and a lot of the time that which is bought remains on the shelf unopened never to be used. Media and marketing companies make use of visuals to market and sell their products as unique or the best in its range. I am not categorizing it as 'bad' merely drawing attention to the fact that it is the system which currently exists and we are all involuntarily tied into the system.

Hopefully I am making you aware of the fact that the companies are the ones creating the need and lack with the consumer using visuals and advertisements. The system of consumerism gave birth to keeping up with your neighbours, the Jones'. In order to be fashionable, trendy and fit in, we just have to acquire the latest and most advanced product available in the market, not thinking about consequences. Marketing companies are creating and driving the need in the minds of men and women.

I am not by any stretch of imagination advocating that you should not drive a lovely new car or live in a beautiful home. I am merely stating a fact that we are being deceived into believing that the latest and newest of everything will make our lives better and happier. This kind of thinking is self-destructive and void of truth. You have the keys within you to be filled with joy and happiness. We all do, and it comes from our state of mind.

I have gotten a bit off the track here and need to regress back to my chain of thought, describing the dynamics of quantum physics. I draw your attention again to the fact that you are quantum even if you do not perceive it. Your spirit and God is connected to all the other Gods on the other side of the veil **(remember: everything is God)**. Only on the physical plane do we see and experience separation from each other.

On the other side of the veil all is one and one is all. The tapestry of God, as I call it, has no limits or boundaries. You are divine and loving; a part of the whole and through becoming human the soul is able to gain valuable knowledge whilst journeying through many lives and many obstacles.

EXPERIENCES IN LIFE TRIGGER EMOTIONS AND FEELINGS

NOW WE ARE GETTING TO the meaty stuff. Are you able to relate to someone how it feels to love another and to have lost your lover to cancer or a disease if you have not been through a similar experience yourself? The answer is 'no'. You may say you have an idea of how the person might feel, but in actual fact you may never know or understand completely until you have gone through the same ordeal yourself. You might sympathize, or even be able to feel empathy for the other person, but this still does not give you the experience of having lost a loved one.

Let's use the example of a couple expecting a baby. The mother bearing the child has a total different experience to her partner with regards to her hormones, emotions and physical transformation. Although some men are conscious and even linked with the mother's emotions and feelings, they will not truly have the same physical experiences. The actual birthing process with labour pains and delivery are impossible to describe to a man. The new born baby is unique and the DNA and genetic makeup comprises that of both parents.

Can you say that you will know how each of the parents must have felt if you have not been through a similar experience? The answer is most definitely not. You might think you know, but in actual fact, until you have experienced having a baby of your own you cannot truly describe the intense, deep love and affection felt by the parents at the birth of their new born.

Even so, each woman going through the birthing experience will not have the same emotions and feelings as her friends or neighbours. There will be those parents who are also less involved than others in raising the young one. Some mothers and fathers might not even be involved at all, as they may have given the baby up for adoption. We cannot judge as we have not walked a single step in those parents' shoes.

Experiences in life trigger emotions and feelings which can either be described as pleasant or unpleasant. These feelings and emotions have a direct link with the frame of mind and consciousness of the individual. Our mind sends a signal to our emotional body, and we react in a certain way when an event or situation occurs. These events are brought into our quantum field by mostly our own thinking. We are the creators of all events and experiences by drawing them into our orbit.

EXPERIENCES ARE ATTRACTED TO US BY THE WAY OF OUR THINKING

THE QUANTUM FIELD IS FOREVER changing and will be forever changing as we are forever changing in the field. You are not the same person you were a few years back – you have changed, evolved and aged. I trust that over time even your thinking has changed, as our thinking habits are fundamental towards creating a life which we desire. If we think negative thoughts, we are setting them into play in the quantum field.

For this very reason we need to monitor our every thought and make sure if we see any negative thoughts appearing in the mind that we immediately change them into positive thoughts. We all have the power to do so; it may take long but all the Masters who ever walked on the earth's plane did just that. They spend years perfecting the art, never allowing for any negative thoughts to taint and contaminant their minds. They are the Master of their minds and they realized long ago that by thinking and focusing on the positive, they will attract only the positive into their lives.

Our brain's neural pathways[23] are programmed and infused with an enormously large collection of patterns in the mother's womb. These run automatically, and it takes years to still the human mind. We are so used to comparing and analyzing

---

[23] Neural pathway: http://en.wikipedia.org/wiki/Neural_pathway

everything on our journey through life, which creates a habit of thinking which is very difficult to break. We learn from our parents and they instil certain beliefs, behaviours and views in us, followed by our teachers and peers who also have an effect on the way we see and live life. The majority of us are never trained to think outside of the box and to only see the 'good and bad' as just a learning experience.

SEE THE POSITIVE IN ALL EMOTIONALLY UNPLEASANT EXPERIENCES IN LIFE

IF OUR PARENTS DRINK HEAVILY, most of the time we will follow suit; or if they are in an abusive relationship, most of the time the kids will follow the same pattern. This, however, is not always the case, as each person has their own distinctive mind-set, and together with their free will is able to make sense and view life as they see fit. Nobody can make you feel bad, sad, ashamed, and happy or loved, if you in your own mind do not decide to feel bad, sad, ashamed, happy or loved. You have full power over everything, determined by your thinking.

So many of us, including myself, choose to see events as negative instead of just seeing them as an experience - nothing more, nothing less. We get hooked on the emotions, struggling to let go of the awful feelings. These painful feelings determine how we will experience a similar situation when a new event unfolds, and we have not learned the lessons from the past by letting go of the old emotions and thinking habits. Our human minds are programmed to replay past memories and keep us trapped in a downward spiral until we decide to break free from the past emotional patterns and triggers.

Let's say for instance that you were in a malicious relationship were your partner cheated on you and your world fell apart.

This experience brought you to a place where you were utterly man-down. It felt like your world had been ripped out from underneath you with nothing more in life to live for.

You either had the option to lie down and play the victim game by saying to all your friends, 'look at what he or she did to me'. Another option could be to retaliate and hit back at the person by hurting and inflicting pain back. The alternative option might be to stand up, accept and own that even in this situation you had a part to play in creating this reality. Even though you may have found the experience to be excruciatingly unpleasant and humiliating, it's important to learn the lesson by heart and take the good out of all experiences in life, better equipped to move forward.

You might say to me that you never created this reality, or ask how you could have played a role in manifesting this reality, since you were not the one who cheated. Well, my friend, it is important to realize that at some level of your consciousness, knowingly or unknowingly, you agreed to go through the experience. Difficult as it may be for you to accept the fact, it remains that you had a part to play in this event. You will now know first-hand how another person will feel if you betrayed them. Hopefully you will therefore think twice before you render such pain and suffering on another human.

Your reaction might be that it is ludicrous or even crazy, but as I pointed out earlier we are all connected on this side of the veil as well as on the other side of the veil. On the other side everything is known to God and all Gods are one God and have a part to play in what we are creating consciously or unconsciously.

You might say, 'nonsense, how can this be?' Your God at all times knows what you are going through. Your Higher Self, your eternal observer self as it is known is always present with you throughout life. I wish to expand on this by referring to your Higher Self, as the Son (or Daughter) of God and part of the Holy Trinity connecting you to God, the Father (or Mother) and the Holy Spirit as explained in the Bible.[24] You are never apart from your God and a piece of your spirit and God is always present with you on the physical side of the veil.

---

[24] Your Higher Self, observer self is also known to many as your God or True Self which is directly linked to God's Mind. Please refer to the New American Standard Bible, New Testament in the book of Matthew 28:19-20 - 19 'Go therefore and make disciples of all the nations, baptizing them in the name of the Father and the Son and the Holy Spirit, 20 teaching them to **observe all** that I commanded you; and lo, I am with you always, even to the end of the age.'.

GOD IS LOVE

THE JOURNEY IS LOVE AND to always love unconditionally. God is pure love and compassion, nothing but love. Part of our journey is to find and unravel this infinite love within ourselves and to see the same deep love within other humans, plants or animals as everything radiates and comes from the love of God. If God is love, then everything in and around our world must also be love.

Love is the nature of our reality, to make known the unknown, to discover our own greatness and magnificence and not to get tied down by life and the betrayals of other people. Just see it as a part of the journey of learning to love more and deeper, **first yourself**, and then others. See each person as trying to do the best with what they know.

I know what you are going to ask me next, 'so why did he or she betray my love?', and 'why did he or she not love me enough?' The answer is: **'love yourself'**. You cannot find love in another before you find love in you. Love does not judge, fear or compare, it simply IS always and will always be. Love is God. God is Love.

Love does not judge, fear or compare,
it simply IS always and will always be.
Love is God. God is Love.

Exercise 5 - Love

Find yourself a mirror you can use for this exercise and place yourself in front of it. What do you see when gazing into the mirror? You see the physical manifestation of a spiritual being. Do you like what you see? Do you love what you see? You are a manifestation of God's perfect love; pure, unconditional, agape love!

Follow this up with saying the words, 'I love you - <u>your name</u>, I really really love you - <u>your name</u>'. Do this over and over, until you start to believe and feel it in your heart. Please do not focus on your ego or image when speaking these words, as the energy being transmitted will be muted, having no influence on your Being. Only use genuine expressions and feelings of love. Next hug yourself affectionately.

This may be tough for some and you may start to weep, because of built up sadness, pain, betrayal, anger and resentment towards yourself. Please do not stop, as this is so normal, and part of learning to love yourself. The first step to enlightenment is to love you - *just the way you are* - as God does.

Now take a deeper look, and this time focus all your attention on your eyes, the seat of your soul. Go ahead and say to your God part, your Higher Self, 'I love you'. Again place your attention on motherly love and affection, until you can feel it deep inside your Being.

By loving yourself more daily, you will intrinsically start to love those around you more. Nothing happens in separation; all processes of life are entangled in the quantum field. Once you are more aware, be more courageous and repeat this process whilst imagining the face of a person you loathe or the face of your greatest adversary in the mirror before you.

THE QUANTUM FIELD CONNECTS ALL PEOPLE, PLACES, TIMES AND EVENTS

IMAGINE FOR A MOMENT THAT your partner has betrayed you and you are at a loss to the rationale for the betrayal. Could it be that you lost yourself and your identity in another person or perhaps in your career resulting in your partner seeking companionship somewhere else? Could it be that your partner's hormones went wild and the electricity was just too difficult to ignore resulting in the betrayal? I spoke about the magnets and how the closer the two get to each other the stronger the pull to connect becomes, eventually leading to their collision.

We live in a world bounded by energy, where every person's frequency and vibration is relative to their consciousness. The whole world is part of the quantum field and each one of us is connected to this energy field or matrix. You are a part of the whole whether you realize it or not. The whole might appear separate but it is not. We are unable to see the connections with the physical eye, but everything is connected with thin invisible threads of energy and particles.

The quantum field connects all people in the world through the mind and is available to you to create your own reality within a greater reality. People, places, times and events are orchestrated in your world and reality for the sole and only purpose to enable to create and experience life. There is a big divine plan and we are unable to comprehend it all – we are merely here to, or ought to, make known the unknown.

Events are created by synchronicity and we are guided by them along the journey of life. This became very apparent to me a few a years ago when I started exploring the true essence of life and existence. I was and still am lead by a force far greater than me, but soon I realized that actually I am part of that force leading and guiding me. I am the designer and creator at the same time.

Every person in your reality was placed there by you – every event in your life was either consciously or unconsciously created and attracted by you to experience life and grow in your understanding of love – to love yourself more and to love the world more.

Our human, practical thinking mind wants to figure out everything and in quantum reality of being human it's impossible to always know what is going to happen next. How boring would life be if we *did* know what was going to happen next – all predictable and nothing to look forward to, no new experiences. You might as well die and return to heaven if that was the case.

The quantum field connecting all of us also relates to the experiences we have requested before being born into the earth's plane, purely because there are valuable life lessons to be learnt. Although this sounds difficult to comprehend, it is the truth.

LAW OF KARMA AND DUALITY
IN THE QUANTUM FIELD

THE FACT THAT WE REQUESTED our experiences before entering the earth plane is even more difficult to understand as there appears to be much turmoil and unrest on the planet today. People are standing up against governments ruled by tyranny and injustices on a daily basis. They want what everyone wants, basic human rights such as food, water, shelter, free education and health.

The earth's energy system has been imbalanced for far too long. Dark energy has been ruling our planet with the intent to enrich the minority and enslave to majority. In saying this I attach no judgment, as it was very necessary for us to experience both sides. Duality always reveals to us two sides of the scale – war and peace, rich and poor, big and small, full and empty, hot and cold, even male and female, with many more opposites present in the program of duality. Add the element of Karma into the mix and that brings about experiences created in the push and pull environment called 'planet earth'.

Each person has a uniquely programmed DNA made up of traits, behaviours and beliefs. These were either received upon entering the earth plane or instilled within you by your parents, friends, teachers or society. Each life before the present has led you to this exact point, with the life lessons and experiences you desired to enable you to grow and evolve. The concept of duality coupled with Karma goes a long way to explain why it is very difficult for a person to break the mould they were born into.

The law of Karma states, 'whatsoever a man soweth, that shall he also reap', or as the Bible teaches, 'In everything, therefore, treat people the same way you want them to treat you, for this is the Law and the Prophets'.[25] Karma always has to be faced and cleared; and the dilemma might arise where in a past life you did something 'bad' and you need to own it in a similar fashion in your current life or the next. The Hindus know and mostly obey the law of Karma, and so too do Buddhists, Taoists and many other religions. As I mentioned earlier, Christians, Jews and Muslims apply the law slightly differently due to the element of 'sin'.

You could have unfinished business from a previous life, and these events will have to play out in your current life, until you free yourself from the crutches of Karma. Our thoughts, words and actions create our reality and in turn have an impact on other people and their reality. Thus Karma is nothing other than cause and effect. Good intent and good deeds contribute to good karma and future happiness, whilst bad intent and bad deeds contribute to bad karma and future suffering.

The soul is on a voyage of evolution through discovery and consequently various principles apply in the workings of the quantum field. Karma and duality are but two of the concepts making up this forever changing quantum field which connects each and every individual.

Another facet of the law of Karma relates closely to placing the sins of the fathers and mothers on the children as

---

[25] New American Standard Bible, New Testament in the book of Matthew 7:12.

mentioned in the Bible.[26] Intrinsically it means that you inherit your parents' DNA and genetic makeup - if they were drug users or alcoholics the same addictions and patterns will almost certainly be apparent in your life. Your quest would therefore be to break the generational chains of addiction.

The law of Duality furthermore refers to the law of 'good and evil', 'light and dark' or 'yin-yang'. The energy force that has dominated in the law of duality over the past few centuries and millennia are, in my view, identifiable as the 'dark and evil' force. This has slowly changed, and from the end of 2012 the 'light and good' side has a slight upper hand.

We, the entire human race as a collective consciousness, have managed to change our planet. We are slowly progressing into a more positive and lighter existence. Our minds, our thinking, our world, *everything* is put together with the concept of 'good and evil'. There is no Satan. Satan was created by man to instil fear for a very long time. I, too, once believed in Satan and going to hell if I 'sinned' and did not repent.

Hell is a state of mind. You find yourself in hell when you compare and feel depressed about your present state or what has happened to you in life. Hell can either be by your own doing or by the hands of another inflicting pain onto you. It is important to note that you always choose to accept the suffering or hell from the other individual (or not). All is a state of mind.

The 'dark and evil' force, if you want to label it as such, has no power if you do not believe in it. Our minds have the

---

[26] New American Standard Bible, Old Testament in the book of Numbers 14:18 - 'The Lord is slow to anger and abundant in loving kindness, forgiving iniquity and transgression; but He will by no means clear the guilty, visiting the iniquity of the fathers on the children to the third and the fourth generations.'.

ability to see everything as a journey and part of life. There are no bad things; they are just there to help you evolve into a higher understanding of life and to enable you to grasp and know that you are ultimately the creator of your own reality and destiny by the way you think, speak and act.

THE REASON BEHIND HARSH
AND DIFFICULT EXPERIENCES

You may pose the questions, 'why are there so many starving and helpless people in the world?' and 'why is there so much bad happening in the form of deaths, hate and unrest all over the world?' My reply simply is that the souls living in these gruelling places have chosen to have these evolutionary experiences as their God is always present in the good and bad times.

A soul might come into the earth plane for a few hours as a baby and die, causing the parents incredible grief. This was an experience created by all parties on the spiritual side of the veil. The parents may have wanted to experience the depth of loss and grief to truly know what love is. The very same soul may enter a year or two down the line and by this time the husband and wife may have a greater appreciation for life and for their newborn baby. There is no wrong and right in the world, only experiences to help you love more.

'I know' this statement puts me in the front row of a firing squad. Well that is my truth; love is everything, whether you label it 'good and bad'. All souls are moving towards finding the truth and love of God inside of them. A Master never judges what people do, whether that person commits murder or slowly kills themselves by being an alcoholic. All Masters are in actual fact incapable of doing so, as they have reprogrammed the part of the brain responsible for judgment. God has given each individual free will and choice, how to act and lead their life. All Masters simply walk by showing the way with love and light.

A person born in a shack or in the slums might not know any better than to beg, borrow or steal to stay alive. That, too, is part of the journey of the soul – the experiences requested by the person to evolve or Karma that has to be faced and cleared.

We should never feel the need to change any person, whoever they are or whatever they are doing. Be the change – show others the way by acting sincerely with compassion and love. Regard every person as a family member, with no regard to their status or way of acting.

Without people there would only be an uninhabited planet with wild animals roaming around. Each person is divine, with the spark of God within them, and their choices and actions guide their distinct life path. We always have a choice in life, whether to beg, borrow or steal, whether to laugh or cry, whether to run or walk. The decision is yours!

THE PUSH AND PULL OF ENERGIES - FORCES OF 'LIGHT AND DARK'

THESE TWO OPPOSING ENERGIES THAT exist, the 'light and dark' are an integral part of the whole system. I mentioned previously that we are constantly evolving; and if that were not the case everything would stay stagnate and the same. That is however and fortunately not the reality: as even a criminal can be transformed for the better.

To return to my quantum theory, the 'dark and evil' side is part and parcel of each and every human being born on planet earth. Our minds have been genetically programmed with the reality of duality. In addition, we have been programmed with the DNA and genetic makeup of our parents, our grandparents, coupled with their patterns, beliefs, views and behaviours. Add the elements of past lives and Karma into the genetic mixture and it becomes clear that a human is created to navigate through life either having challenging experiences or wonderful opportunities.

'Dark' is relative to each individual and person. The dark force can be so strong and overpowering that the human mind is controlled, resulting in one human stealing, raping or even killing another member of the family. The energy pull created by the forces of 'light and dark' brings human beings into contact allowing for the experience to unfold consciously or unconsciously. Yet, part of you is always aware of the existence of all possibilities and potentials.

That part is your Higher Self, your God part that is always present with you on the physical and spiritual sides of the veil and connects you to each and every human on the planet. These events are all known potentials and nothing happens by chance. All seemingly random events are a part of the synchronicity being played out as God's divine plan.

It is crucial to emphasize the overwhelming power of the 'dark and evil' force consuming the individual's human mind and leading to irrational acts without considering the consequences of their actions. The reaction is immediate, instinctive and sometimes extremely difficult to control or change.

Using the analogy of colliding magnets, the closer 'dark and evil' force venture towards each other the more difficult it is to stay apart. We have all had the experience of losing our 'cool' and lashing out at another person and instantly regretting it, wishing we could take it back. Many of us have experienced an incident or two where the anger and rage became so overpowering we passed the point of no return – just open a newspaper or switch on the television – it happens on a daily basis.

What is the origin of these acts and behaviours, where do they come from? These acts are triggered by our human mind's programming and the way we perceive the world. Being on the recipient end of somebody else's hurt and anger, might be the result of something 'bad' done by you in a previous life and just Karma manifesting itself in this lifetime.

It is important to find a release for the stored and bottled up negative emotions and feelings and to free ourselves from past hurt and pain. I suggest go for a walk in nature and scream at the top of your lungs if you feel the need to release blocked energy of emotions; you could write a letter to the individual who harmed you and afterwards burn the letter – by watching the smoke and ashes release the hurt and anger to God; cry, hit a punching bag – whatever works for you in a safe way to release the blocked emotions. Then move forward without glancing over your shoulder to the past.

QUANTUM LIVING MEANS LIVING THE PRESENT FOREVER IN THE NOW

ALTHOUGH MY TEACHING MAY BE a little intense, it is important to know that everything is about increasing your light and saying 'no' to the dark, however difficult this may be. Living with integrity not only relates to our actions, but also to our thoughts and spoken words. We need alignment of thought, word and deed, the alignment of a Master Being with no Karma and living only in the present with no past or future. This state of mind means that we will continuously and forever experience the future in the now, a fully quantum being, where our spirit and God has claimed the 'Christ', 'God-man' realized.

Master Beings realize within them that they have the power to create and manipulate the quantum field to create a reality and bring forth any experience their God so desires. They are at one with making known the unknown and continue to conjure a new dream, and then create reality from the dream.

Start to understand that the present moment is all we have – the future does not exist and the past is gone. We cannot relive the past, so why, then, do we think so much about our past experiences? This is because our past experiences have trapped us, and we have failed to see the truth – that they were just there to help us grow. We need to free our emotions from past experiences and not let them chain and shackle us in the present.

If emotions are holding you back, you still have not passed the lesson with flying colours and until you do so, a similar experience will keep returning into your orbit until you do learn the lesson from that particular experience. Then you can say, 'enough, I have learned my lesson and now move forward in life'.

As mentioned earlier, the quantum field is an energy field with an unlimited amount of potentials and possibilities simultaneously existing. Every particle of our being is energy, and that energy vibrates at a frequency. Your frequency and vibration depend on your view of yourself, your beliefs and attitudes, it is your consciousness. The more you see yourself and everything as God, the higher you will start to vibrate. This is the path from involution to evolution. We come from light and we are here to find our way back to light and God. The light is within each one of us. The great Masters realized their divine light.

The journey is a beautiful one and much hard work is needed to embrace and change any negative thoughts and habits. As we let go of old debilitating emotions from past experiences, we start to liberate the mind and more freedom will manifest itself every step of the way. Monitoring our thinking is the key, being the eternal observer self and able to see the games our human mind plays. Every person embarking on a spiritual journey will have ups and downs as there is no easy fix, it's a lifetime of monitoring your thoughts and changing the negative thoughts into positive thoughts.

Hopefully it will not take so long, and I say this with a big smile. Every time you embrace, change and let go of a taxing experience, the light inside you will shine brighter.

More people will start to see how life is unfolding and honour you for your actions. More good things will just happen at random – no – there is no such thing as random; you will start to experience more joyous synchronicity.

Your intuition will start to guide you through life and you will more clearly start to hear the voice inside your heart speaking to you. The quantum field will help you create whatever you put your mind to, and the choice is yours whether you are going to listen or ignore what is unfolding. The communication channels to God are always open and all you and I have to do is tune in to the frequency and listen.

I might not be aware of everything that the Masters see and know, but from my own experiences and learning to date I know the master plan is to become a quantum God, forever present in the now, by creating and living experiences through every thought that manifests itself.

YOUR THOUGHTS AND ACTIONS
HAVE KARMIC CONSEQUENCES

As WE ARE NEVER SEPARATE from God, we are all divinely guided by God. We are all Gods, although most of the world has yet to come to this realization. Our thoughts and actions have an effect on other human beings. You always have a choice how you want to treat someone even if that someone treated you poorly. You can either walk away or retaliate, the choice is yours.

Having said this, know that you always have the right to defend yourself if someone wants to inflict bodily harm on you in times when you are met with face-to-face confrontation. You may always use the necessary and appropriate means to protect yourself and another person from receiving any bodily harm. Nobody should ever be beaten or kicked in any way as violence is never the answer in any circumstance and the perpetrator will always have to face the Karmic consequences for his or her actions. Aikido is a Japanese martial art created by Ueshiba's, his goal was to formulate an art that practitioners could use to defend themselves while also protecting their attacker from injury.[27]

Having regard to Karmic consequences, it remains unfortunate that most people still continue to lash out at their

---

[27] See Aikido: http://en.wikipedia.org/wiki/Aikido

fellow humans beings. One should realize that even as much as a negative thought projected at another human gives rise to the forces of Karma. The concept is challenging and it requires years of practice to learn and master – never to take anything personally and not to react hastily.

CREATING YOUR DREAMS
STARTS WITH THE MIND

THE QUANTUM FIELD OF ALL possibilities and potentials is available to you to make your dreams come true, whether the dream entails owning your own home, buying a new car or changing careers.

All creations and manifestations have its origin in the mind; the thought is then placed into the quantum field to realize the experience. The secret is always to stay present with what you are doing, then to focus on attracting the new desires into your life; no wrongs or rights – pure creation at its best.

Let's use the example of you acquiring a new car. By the mind contemplating owning a new car, thoughts are being sent into the quantum field. If you are able to hold the thought clearly in your mind's eye, without any attachments, it will arrive and be given to you. As it is stated by Jesus in the Bible, 'And all things you ask in prayer, believing, you will receive'.[28] You need to make known to yourself and to God that you have no idea how this is going to happen, but know that it will take place. Release the 'how' and the timeframe – this is God's department.

---

[28] New American Standard Bible, New Testament in the book of Matthew 21:22 or two parallel quotes are Matthew 7:7 – 'Ask, and it will be given to you; seek and you will find; knock, and it will be opened to you.' and Luke 11:9 – 'So I say to you, ask, and it will be given to you; seek, and you will find; knock, and it will be opened to you.'.

You have now set in motion a sequence of events enabling you to receive the beautiful new car envisaged by you. The universe might offer you a new job or you may receive a promotion creating access to more money to enable you to afford the new car. Take action, be patient and leave the rest up to God and the quantum field. There should be no shadow of a doubt in your mind that it might not realize, or else this process will not work. Envision and believe that you already have the new car, otherwise nothing will happen. Open your heart, by feeling the new car into life, whilst seeing the new car clearly in your reality. Follow this up with feelings of deep gratitude and appreciation to your God. Trust in God always.

We are all Gods, and each one of us is navigating our way back to greatness. We are working the light spectrum, and by staying focused in the present, we are letting go of our old ways and habits. Stop looking to the past, and stay focused in the here and now by being open to synchronicity.

Your new job could be the result of a synchronistic event, like going to a party, a gathering or a function where you end up meeting a person who will offer you the job, or where you were might be introduced to a career recruiter assisting you with finding your dream job. Expect the unexpected *always* – have patience, learn to listen and receive, observe and act.

There is no dream too big or mountain too high, every possibility exists and you have the full right to enjoy every moment of life. We are all guided by our divine connection to God. We just need to listen and hear the call from our ever-present higher being that is assisting us with creating and enjoying our experience. It is important to note that even in synchronicity, we are required to take action in order to meet new people and open the doors of opportunity for that new position, or whatever you want to achieve. We must be open and listen to our intuitive thoughts.

Exercise 6 – Creation and manifestation

Step 1 – Think of something you desire and want to create and attract into your reality, for example a promotion, a new car, a new home, a new painting, finishing a marathon, an overseas trip, or receiving a gorgeous bunch of flowers; whatever that might be for you. Remember, the whole of life is based upon the manifestation of pure intent with no reference to size or scale.

Step 2 – Spend a few minutes every morning as you wake up and every evening before going to sleep, visualizing and focusing in your 'mind's eye'[29] on that which you want to attract into your life. Early mornings are the best as your mind is still clear from any of our daily distractions. Visualization and focusing your mind's eye before falling asleep is of vital importance as you are programming your Higher Self or subconscious mind with your desire, and in doing so, you are leaving the program running in the quantum field which connects all people, places, times and events necessary to create and manifest your desire even if you are asleep. I would suggest that you even draw your desire on a small card, focusing on the card every morning and evening; also position the card so that it may be visible to your subconscious mind at all times.

Step 3 – Whilst visualizing, start feeling how you would be enjoying the promotion, your new car, your new home,

---

[29] Located directly in the centre of your forehead. Also known as your Third Eye and the Sixth Chakra.

your new painting, running and finishing the marathon, your overseas trip or receiving the lovely bunch of flowers. With your sensing and feeling the desire you are sending powerful signals of energy into the quantum field filled with possibilities and infinite potential to create and manifest your desire.

Step 4 - Follow this up with feelings of deep gratitude and appreciation for receiving the promotion, your new car, your new home, your new painting, etc. By focusing with the mind's eye on the desire, and combining the focus with the feelings of joy and gratitude, you are creating a powerful energy link of manifestation between mind and heart. You are feeling your desire into life.

Step 5 - Your next step is to make known to yourself and to God that you have no idea how this is going to happen, but know it will take place. Release the 'how' and the timeframe - this is for God to take care of. Be patient and leave the rest up to God and the quantum field of infinite potential and possibilities.

Step 6 - Lastly, take action, as nothing in life happens without action. Action could be in the form of applying for the promotion, going for the interview or writing an entrance exam by applying your knowledge in order to receive the promotion. Most acts of creation and manifestation will entail action from your part. The nature of action required from you will be revealed to you.

If you can think it you can have it...
You just need to believe it in your heart.

WE ARE ALL GODS OF THE DIVINE HUMAN FAMILY

ALTHOUGH THE QUANTUM FIELD DOES not always make sense, it attracts to us exactly what we created or need to learn to grow as human being. Letting go of all old emotions is a big part of the journey as we walk through life, aiming to look through the eyes of God and not our human eyes. Your 'observer self', or Higher Self, walks with you everywhere; the unseen part of you which connects you to the entire planet, is with you always.

A small number of people have been able to open the filters of their eyes by changing their brain's neural pathways. They are able to look at you and examine your body and see your chakras and aura – the energy centres and bands spinning around your body. Foremost we are spiritual beings living a physical reality – the body is just our image and holds together a small part of who we are. We are so much more than flesh and blood, and the time for remembrance is now.

It is very unfortunate and limiting that most people are still stuck on the outer appearances of others. Over the years society has been conditioning and dictating to us what a person should look and be like. This remains a difficult pattern to break – not to see the outer but to see the inner first. When we meet someone for the first time we somehow scrutinize them from head to toe, formulating opinions based on the person's outward physical appearance. I include myself in this category of people.

I am working hard to change and break my human mind's programming. Difficult as it may be, we can all change the brain's neural pathways, to see 'the Christ' first, before anything else. All people are divine and have 'the Christ' living in them, it may be hidden deep, but it's always present within them. The real truth is for you to see the beauty in both the inner and outer appearances of all people. If you can do this you have arrived home and are at one with how God views all.

We live in a world that looks at the physical beauty of people and although there is nothing wrong with this, it is very limiting. I challenge you at your next encounter with another person to ignore the physical outer appearance but to look deeper – endeavour to catch a glimpse of the divine love and divinity that is present in that human being, and every other human being, no matter their status or outer appearance. Bear in mind that even they might be totally unaware of their divinity because of their traditions, beliefs, views, value systems or years of upbringing which might not acknowledge this divinity.

Life has so much to offer each and every individual. We all have a role to play to make this world a world where only peace, unity, harmony, joy and prosperity exist. Look at your fellow divine family members – it is the person walking down the street, it is the person serving you at the corner shop, it is your fellow passenger on the bus and, yes, it is even your irritating and obnoxious colleague at the office. We are all part of one another, bonded by invisible threads of energy – these threads connect us to the other side of the veil, to a family far larger and greater than our human mind can even begin to imagine.

The Bible refers to this energy or quantum field as the Holy Spirit connecting all people, places, times and events. As we find written in Corinthians; 'but just as it is written, 'THINGS WHICH EYE HAS NOT SEEN AND EAR HAS NOT HEARD, AND which HAVE NOT ENTERED THE HEART OF MAN, ALL THAT GOD HAS PREPARED FOR THOSE WHO LOVE HIM.' For to us God revealed them through the Spirit; for the Spirit searches all things, even the depths of God'.[30] The Holy Spirit binds all things together as God, exploring and seeking the depth of God's love.

The journey involves learning to love each and every person the same, no matter if they are a murderer, thief, prostitute, judge, accountant or policeman. A major purpose of life is to awaken and see the good and God in every person, looking past their background, beliefs or social status. We are all family and part of the body of God. Imagine for a moment a world where access to basic sanitation, health, education, water, food and housing is available and free for all to enjoy, where the earth's water is unpolluted and nature is nurtured for being a part of us. Can you hold this dream in your mind's eye? If you can, you are putting the ball in motion by starting to create the dream where heaven really is a place on earth.

Consciousness works exactly in this manner. Collectively we can create a world where there is no more famine, diseases or lack; a world where love, peace and happiness reign supreme. This world does exist and we all have a role to play, by holding the dream close and dear to our hearts, and by visualizing it with firm intent in our minds' eyes. Do not expect someone else to dream this dream for you, they cannot!

---

[30] New American Standard Bible, New Testament in the book 1 Corinthians 2:9–10.

Collectively we are much stronger than standing by ourselves. There is strength in unity; it has the power to manifest faster than ever before. This is how the quantum field works; we must project and visualize the dream as if it is already a reality. We must see it clearly, believe and feel that we, and the entire human family, are already living in this beautiful and magical Garden of Eden.

DIFFERENT LEVELS OF HUMAN CONSCIOUSNESS

THE DARK AND NEGATIVE PART of energy changes slowly, so very slowly. Just think how a few hundred years ago slave trade was a respected job and nobody saw anything wrong with having a slave; on the contrary it was the norm. Having a slave was almost as natural as having a pet in your garden. The mind did not see anything wrong with the model, until a consciousness started to develop that saw the indignity and inhumane element of having slaves. Equality for every human being was eventually born and with that nationality, race, gender and skin colour become irrelevant.

We still have a road to travel in equality where women are in certain societies still regarded as lower and must be subservient to men. I recently attended a Christian wedding service where I listened to the vows in disbelief as the wife-to-be, vowed to be subservient and look after her spouse. She must almost report to him as though she is second class. The way many Christians interpret the Bible is that the wife is lower in standing than her husband. Most Asian, Eastern, Middle Eastern and African countries have an even more prejudiced view of the female gender. It is, however, important to realize that nobody is higher or lower than anyone else. Equality in every form is the key for evolving and shifting the entire planet into a new paradigm.

Equality is a mind-set and must be cultivated in every human alive today. Only you have the power to change your point of view, nobody can do it for you. Treat people as you want to be treated. Give as you want to receive - unconditionally. Be and allow others to be, live with no limits, and re-program your mind to see the bigger picture by releasing any limiting views and beliefs you've been holding onto. Know all experiences were there to help you grow and discover the true essence of who you are: *a star, a light brighter than the sun, a God.*

Your level of acceptance is based on your level of consciousness and determines your vibration and frequency. Acceptance sets you free and increases your light, and in doing so you are helping the whole planet and the collective consciousness of humanity. In quantum physics, if one particle changes all particles change. One person has the capability to have a huge cumulative effect on the masses holistically; just look at Buddha, Jesus, and Muhammad. It is incredible to think that three of the four major world religions are all less than 2500 years old.

The human beings who sit on the streets and beg, live in the slums or dilapidated shacks, are souls who chose to go through these bleak experiences. This is equally true for people living with physical disabilities or who suffer from malnutrition, living in poor under fed countries where they are starving; these are all souls who have chosen these experiences even if they are not consciously aware of it. These souls chose their body and life in order to grow and go through these excruciating, challenging experiences. Their Higher Self likely wants to learn what suffering is all about. The spirit and soul is immortal and cannot die. The soul is building an array of life knowledge and wisdom every step along the way.

There is no need to feel sorry or bad for the soul ever, it wants to evolve into higher paradigms of existence and has to start from the bottom, building the foundation of its light spectrum. In saying this I realize the journey in life can at times be very strenuous and taxing, but it is not our duty or task to rescue any person along the way. We are here to shine our light and by doing so we create the desire for others to do the same. All souls are here to evolve into a higher understanding of knowledge and wisdom about themselves.

The path of each soul is different, as are the subjective lessons required to be learned by each soul. As such it is important not to force your view onto another or to rescue them. I am by no stretch of any imagination suggesting that you cannot support or show empathy. I am merely alluding to the fact that each soul chose their life and their essential life lessons to grow in awareness and consciousness. We are always able to support and guide each soul to their highest ideal, but it is not in our power, nor is it our place, to take the life lessons away which they have come to experience and learn from.

We must show love and empathy always, be loving and caring to all, as some lessons can be very demanding and complex. Each soul has the ability to stand strong and create for them a beautiful reality in the world to be experienced. It is not for us to judge another's journey, as you may have experience exactly that in a past life. In life there are no winners and losers, there are only the ones participating and the ones sitting on the side-line watching.

GIVING AND RECEIVING IS THE NATURAL FLOW OF ENERGY IN LIFE

BE OPEN AND ALWAYS GIVE of yourself and in doing so even more will be returned to you by the universe and God. The law of giving and receiving applies to all avenues of life and in so doing - a flow of energy is created. Although it may be challenging for some to give, and for some to receive; be aware that this flow of energy is part of life. It is important to give, but also to receive without thinking and analyzing, just do them when the urge and feeling arises.

Too often we start to question the feeling and start contemplating in our minds, debating whether or not to allow ourselves to give. By doing so we are blocking the flow of energy. To allow the energy to become a free flowing river, when you give, give with a whole and open heart and when you receive, receive gracefully with sincerity.

From personal experience I know how challenging it is to break the beliefs and habits of expecting something in return when you give, or feeling indebted when you receive a gift. Let go of that, or else you are blocking the energy flow from the universe to the giver. The giver may receive from another 'source' or in a different unexpected manner in what they need. It could be in the form of their receiving a free massage or someone buying them a beer or paying for their dinner - something is always returned to the giver.

You must just give when you feel your gut and intuition is telling you to do so. By doing so you are opening yourself up to the universal flow of energy. There is an abundance of energy and support available throughout God's majestic creation, just allow for the flow of energy to carry on through you, do not block it.

When you think you want to give to a person, know this is your God-thought and honour the thought by giving to the person. Do not start to analyze your thoughts by thinking, 'how can I give, as I do not have enough money', or, 'who will give back to me?' Have faith in the various universal laws of giving and receiving, Karma, cause and effect, and duality's 'push and pull', as all of these relate to flow of energy. Allow the energy to flow and have the law of giving and receiving create abundance in all forms in your life, from money, to joy, to love and much more.

Enjoy the gift of receiving, and enjoy the gift of giving as both of these are vital and tremendously gratifying. Surrender your thinking and just allow the flow of energy to guide your every feeling and action.

Exercise 7 – Giving and receiving

What are the principles of giving and receiving? There are none, just do it!

What are the different kinds of giving that you can perform in life? You can give of your energy and presence; in the form of time, expertise and labour. You can give money, donations or gifts, such as a free holiday, a free seminar, a free dinner or others. You can give affection and kindness in the form of smiles, hugs, kisses, and more. All forms of giving relate to aspects of love in action as compassion.

What are the various forms of receiving we can experience? As you give, so you shall receive. The world will always mirror to you, that what you sincerely give!

Now, out of the depth of your heart, without expecting anything back, go and do something big or small for a person, animal or plant. Next time you receive a gift, just thank the giver with gratitude and sincerity without feeling obliged to give something in return. Let your energy flow freely.

THE IMPORTANCE OF DAILY FOCUS
AND MIND-FULL PRACTICES

LIFE CAN BE TOUGH AT times, but so worthwhile when you start to liberate yourself from the human mind and all the thoughts that keep you trapped. Not only daily focus, prayer and meditation, but also incorporating other spiritual practices is imperative to becoming aware of negative and repetitive thoughts and actions. Firstly focus on awareness, and then focus on changing the negative thoughts into positive ones. You attract into your life the very things you are thinking about and thus the mind is the most important muscle in the body and requires daily training.

We create from our minds and thus our minds require daily training to be navigated towards a greater good for ourselves and for the whole. Everything that you possess in life is a direct result of your thoughts and how you went about manifesting them into the physical reality. In life you need to believe and know anything is possible when you create from your heart's desire. All of life is about pure intent.

Never allow anyone to say it's impossible and never allow for doubt to creep in. Focus as though you have already received the gift, written the book or started the company. See the reality existing clearly in your mind's eye.

There are times when we think we have been gifted with a great idea or product, only to find that the world does not share our view. Trust and follow your intuition, the messages and visions will come from your spirit and God. Open yourself up to the greater power, ask for guidance and have that power guide you. Your creation should always be open to change as nothing stays the same. Progression is vital in all avenues of life, with faster and more efficient methods constantly coming into life. Imagination and intuition are the drivers by inspiring us to create new art forms, products and inventions.

Never allow for any distraction to sneak in. Focus as if you have completed the race. You can then enjoy the journey taking you towards achieving your goal. Know the quantum field holds the potential to create anything you put your mind to. Your initial idea might have had some flaws or needs some tweaking. Go ahead and modify, adapt and shape your art, firstly to make you happy and then your clients. Some ideas or concepts can take years to develop and even longer to be accepted by audiences and consumers. Persist until you find your winning formula and enjoy the ride getting there.

Every person on the planet is creating every second of the day with their thoughts, words and actions. What are you creating? What do you want to create? You need to decide for yourself and then pursue your dream. My heart's desire is to be one with my God and all my efforts are placed on creating a oneness reality. That means to be present every second of the now, living the future forever in the now.

YOUR HIGHER SELF IS CONNECTED TO THE MIND OF GOD

MANY DIFFERENT REALITIES EXIST AND no-one is more important than the next person. Collectively we are all part of the reality and consciousness of mankind and at the same time we have our own reality and consciousness. All roads ultimately lead to a higher awareness of self, our neighbours and the world we live in.

No person has the same reality, views and beliefs. You can show various people the same object and each person will describe the object differently and according to how *they* see it. Their human mind will use language and words familiar to them in order to describe the attributes and facts of the object.

Truth differs for each person and therein lies another key of quantum magic, because as our truth changes so does our love. We are continuously evolving and expanding as we accept greater aspects of who we are; by not denying any part, but embracing all parts of who we are. Allow for expansion and creation to fill your every atom and cell, feel it and know you are being guided towards far greater heights than ever imaginable.

'Quantum living' means the connection to all things and people; everything is connected in the entire universe. Nothing is outside of this scope as all form part of God. Yes, Source is everything that ever has been, is and will be. This is the plain and simple reality of quantum physics. It is simple to understand and at the same time so very complicated to comprehend for our limited and analytical human minds.

We need to let go of the conditioned human mind and move more into alignment with our Higher Self; this consciousness is always present as our observer self and follows us wherever we go. Your Higher Self is connected to the Mind of God, the quantum field of infinite potentials - where we receive intuitive thoughts and messages. In actual fact, you and all humans are both Higher Self and God-Mind as we are nothing and everything, the quantum entanglement and interconnectedness of all life.

Let us stand still for a brief moment and exam the above paradox: 'we are nothing and everything'. Everything starts from nothing as nothingness comes before thought. You being human and alive today have evolved from nothing to everything that you currently think you are. Think of it this way, before your parents had the thought of making you - you where nothing. Thus, everything that you are today is a direct result of nothingness which later by way of thoughts manifested itself into physical reality.

Our Higher Self part is connected to the spiritual side of the veil and assists us with creating our reality. We must learn to follow our gut, our intuition or our sixth sense which is always present within all people. The problem rests in the fact that most of the world is still disconnected and not able listen to their Higher Self as they operate from a human mind perceptive. They only see the physical world, making it difficult for them to believe in the spiritual aspects and the quantum field of reality.

Nothing escapes the quantum field and even if you do not believe me, all is known to God or Source. This includes every cell and fibre of your being, from the smallest particle to the greatest part of who you are. You are far more than the physical body. You are connected to all that is, has been and ever will be. This is called *'the oneness principle'* and the core of quantum magic.

Your observer or Higher Self travels with you everywhere and allows for you to do whatever you feel you would like to experience, from eating an ice cream, to meeting up with a friend and having a party. You cannot be alone as your Higher Self is ever-present with you. Your Higher Self is ready to connect with you at anytime, and all you need to do is be still and listen to your intuitive thoughts and messages. These thoughts and messages will come to you in due time from the spiritual side of the veil.

We are always guided by spirit and God and all we need to do is tune in and listen to our intuition. Intuition will guide you to places where synchronicity and events will start to multiply in an ever-expanding universe. Start listening to the God part of which you are, the part that does not always makes sense, the part connected to all other humans on the planet and arranges for synchronicity to occur and magical events to take place.

How can we distinguish between our God and our ego voices? For most of us this can be especially tricky, as sometimes the voice of the ego disguises itself as the voice of God. To do this, let's refer back to exercise three and four where we worked with your current thoughts and judgments. Which part of your being is judging? Your human mind. Your ego is the loud voice in your head responsible for judging, comparing and analyzing all aspects of life from morning to night. Your human mind with the help of the ego is on auto-pilot.

The inner voice of God, your Higher Self is much softer and quieter, completely non-judgmental. This intuitive voice can be associated with pure inspiration or a knowingness from deep within your being. The messages sent from God's Mind to the Higher Self do not have any conditions attached to them, do not seek to criticize, belittle or tear down any person or anything, and do not seek validation or acknowledgment. These messages are flashes of insight fuelled by passion and encouragement built on a fountain of truth and love.

THE AURIC FIELD IS THE BODY'S INVISIBLE BUBBLE OF ENERGY

SEE YOURSELF SURROUNDED BY AN invisible bubble of light. This bubble is your auric field. Your aura consists of invisible energy bands spinning around the physical body called your 'quantum' or 'spiritual body'. Your spiritual body holds your DNA and genetic patterning, linking to the physical body. The spiritual body has seven major energy centres, called 'chakras', and from them flows thousands of 'nadis' all over our physical body connecting the spiritual and physical bodies. These nadis are the channels responsible for the flow of energy and consciousness throughout the body as the physical body is run by the quantum you.

The above is the reason why most Eastern and Asian religious teachings like Buddhism, Hinduism, Taoism and others use practices to unlock these energy centres so energy and consciousness can flow freely throughout your whole body. They use methods and disciplines such as Yoga, Tai Chi, Qigong, Tantra, Aikido, Jujutsu and many more connecting to or using life-force energy depending on the discipline. Some aid in the flow of energy to heal the body, whilst other practices use the attackers' energy to defend them.

Another healing discipline making use of many of the nadis to heal people is the traditional Chinese method of acupuncture. Acupuncture is a collection of procedures which involves penetration of the skin with the help of needles to stimulate specific points on and in the body. The acupuncture practitioners use these acupuncture points in order to balance the yin and yang[31] and flow of chi[32] through channels known as meridians (also known as nadis), these points connect both the physical and spiritual bodies.

See this energy bubble around you as part of your Higher Self and your innate[33] as the link between the your physical and spiritual bodies. If you are able to alter your light or spiritual body in any way, you also alter the physical body, as they are intertwined as one. Your innate can been seen as the chakras and nadis linking these bodies which are ultimately driven by your Higher Self.

When you start to move into the observer, or Higher Self, you have the ability to alter at will that which you choose to. The spiritual presence of the observer self is not visible with the naked eye and is seated slightly behind your head or brain area; your Higher Self waiting to be activated to take over the reins and control of the body once the human thinking mind subsides and dies.

The death of the human thinking mind causes an influx of energy and awareness to your brain and your Higher Self to take full control over every aspect of who you are. In your bubble there is now an abundance of energy available to create and even change your appearance from old to young. You are no longer bound by time as all time is now. You understand that your energy is everywhere and nowhere at the same time. You know the truth about life and enjoy a rich life, wandering the cosmos at your will.

---

[31] Yin and Yang are two opposing forces that are interconnected and interrelated in the world, much like the natural duality – 'dark and light'. http://en.wikipedia.org/wiki/Yin_and_yang

[32] Chi is mostly translated as to 'breath' or 'air' or even natural energy and life-force energy.

[33] Your innate can also be seen as your inborn or intuitive part forming the bridge between your physical and spiritual bodies.

Picture 1 – The Chakras and Nadis

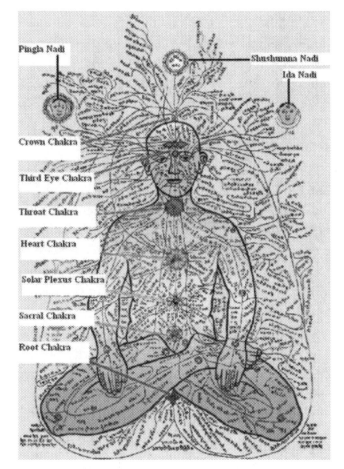

Source reference: http://www.thehealersbible.com/nadis.html

ALL ELEMENTS OF LIFE
HAVE A CONSCIOUSNESS

YOUR SPIRIT IS FAR LARGER than you can ever begin to imagine, and all you have to do is open up and connect to your Higher Self and allow for the magic to happen around every corner. The plants, trees and animals are all part of who you are – nothing is separate from you quantumly. When you become the observer self and start to tune in you will understand what I say. There is a deeper consciousness connection between all living things on the planet and you are a part of them as much as they are a part of you.

Have you seen how people can talk to dogs, horses and dolphins? I presume you have, and as a result can agree to all living life as having a consciousness, being alive and able to be spoken to. Even the plants, trees and water are conscious. There have been a number of experiments done on water and when crude language and emotions are used the water loses crystal structure and turns foul. On the other hand, when words of love and peace are used, the water can turn from foul to clean, and as a result display an array of exquisitely beautiful crystals visible under a microscope. The frequency and vibration of the water is affected by the thoughts of people, as even water is conscious and responds to people's emotions and feelings.[34]

---

[34] See Doctor Masaru Emoto, website: http://www.masaru-emoto.net/english/water-crystal.html

It is interesting to think that our use of language and attitude can affect almost any living and breathing form of life. We have the power to create from this point and need to be aware of all our thoughts, words and deeds, as they have a great effect on the whole, good or bad.

The same applies to all animals and plants. All living organisms have a consciousness and awareness and can be interacted with and spoken to. I have personally seen how my mother lovingly speaks to her plants and vegetables. These vegetables grow bigger and taste more succulent than the ones you would buy at the supermarket or grocer. There is indeed magic inside every living organism and we need to treat all life with respect, honour and dignity.

Have you ever eaten free-range eggs? If not, take pleasure in having the experience. Recently I visited a couple of friends on a farm nearby where each chicken had been given a name and funny enough responds to his or her name. I know how bizarre this may sound, but it remains the truth. I was given two eggs laid by these chickens roaming freely for breakfast and they are by far the best eggs I have eaten in my life. These eggs were so succulent and tasty, truly heavenly.

Are you starting to see the bigger picture? Can you start to imagine the invisible thread of energy connecting all living parts even the plants, trees and animals on the earth? Best you start to imagine and begin to comprehend this truth. As the connection and consciousness of humanity grows on the planet, so will this aspect become clearer for all to witness and recognize in the future. Very much as we see illustrated in the blockbuster movie Avatar, all elements of life are consciously interconnected and related.

We came down from the plane of bliss to make known the unknown, and in doing so we are here to experience all aspects of life and grow into higher dimensions and paradigms of awareness. The earth knows more than we do and is here to support and be of service to the whole, responding to our vibration and frequency. The earth, too, is a living organism, responsible for all life and containing divine mother wisdom. All we need to do is look around and see how the birds, plants, trees and insects continue to live and thrive on their own, without any need from us humans.

The quantum field of consciousness is always present, that divine connection linking all living organisms. Indeed, it is the magic thread that weaves us all together, and it does not matter who you are, where you come from or what you do. The collective consciousness and *oneness principle* is a truth.

AIR IS FILLED WITH VITAL LIFE-FORCE ENERGY

I WANT YOU TO GO outside, feel the wind in your hair and for those with no hair feel it on your skin. Look around you. Can you see the wind? No, you cannot; but it's there in the form of leaves being whisked away, or by the swaying movement of the trees as the wind caresses the branches. The wind is air, ever-present and an essential food for all life.

There is energy in the air, vital life-force energy. Why do you think all trees need air? All plants need air, and almost all living organisms require the oxygen in the air. Even the fish in the ocean use oxygen to breathe and survive. Energy resides in air and is much needed for humans, animals and plants to live and survive. A person will pass on within a few minutes if they do not receive air, as the brain needs oxygen to work and perform the bodily functions.

Why do you think so many spiritual practices involve or require focusing on the breath? Various disciplines from a mixture of meditations, such as Yoga, Tai Chi, Qigong, and many more all understand the importance of air and the connection with the breath. There is vital life-force energy in air that can elevate an individual into a higher dimension or paradigm, a natural trance-like state. Actually, we have forgotten how to get there, and these practices assist us by letting go of the 'monkey-mind' or auto-pilot, and help us to focus on one object or on nothing, increasing our awareness and connection to all life.

A normal state of joy and euphoria may arise from practicing these disciplines; it however depends on the individual, their focus and dedication to the practice. A vastness from within and connectedness to all life arises when the erratic and uncontrolled thinking mind subsides. This erratic and uncontrolled thinking mind is known to most Buddhists as your 'monkey-mind'. We have lost our connection to this normal state of bliss and joy. We cannot go there with the human thinking mind, and instead, need to become the observer self by raising the energy and consciousness within our body.

Joy is a natural state of existence, and the physical wellbeing provided by these practices is astronomical and surpasses normal running, cycling or swimming. Even science is waking up and investigating the phenomenon of vital life-force energy present in air; when you start to focus on the chi energy, you become aware of this ever-present force, ready to be harnessed and used by the practitioner.

Even running can be transformed into an activity that brings on greater highs than ever before when intent and focus is placed on the breath by connecting with chi. Most runners exercise because they receive not only the benefits of looking more youthful and healthy, but it also gives them a natural high called the 'runners high'. The runner's high is brought on by the release of endorphins which are produced in the brain by the pituitary gland and the hypothalamus in vertebrates during intense exercise. It has also been suggested that apart from endorphins, other neurotransmitters can contribute to a runner's high; and these include epinephrine, serotonin and dopamine.[35] Runners live to experience this daily high as it increases alertness, brain function and makes them feel happier. You can try to achieve this greater 'high' by running and concentrating on your every in and out breath, and connecting with the expansiveness of your surroundings.

For me there are two main states or pillars of running which are linked to mediation; the one is to think of nothing – 'no human-mind', otherwise called 'the zone', and the other is to focus on everything and be aware of your surroundings. Each is vitally important for those persons wanting to expand and grow spiritually. The first pillar is to slow down the 'monkey-mind', and the next to increase the awareness and the connectedness to all life. The law of averages apply, and thus the more you practice the two principles the better you will get at connecting with the chi, stilling the 'monkey-mind' and expanding your awareness. Go for it, start running!

---

[35] Runner's high: http://en.wikipedia.org/wiki/Endorphins

THE CREATIVE POWER
OF ALL WORDS

WHERE TO NEXT, YOU MIGHT ask? You can choose anyplace and anywhere you would like to explore. You are the driver and are navigating the planet through your thoughts, words and actions. Words are paramount, and many humans misuse the power of the spoken word. When you speak you create a quantum effect, whether it is neutral, good or bad. Words have tremendous power and have a binding effect by creating a reality for the individual speaking the words. You must always watch your words and take care when uttering them.

Nothing in the quantum field goes unnoticed; everything has an effect on the whole, either for the good or for the bad. You have heard the old saying, 'my words have come back to bite me in the ass'. This is so true! Many words are spoken idly and cause a ripple effect on the whole. Watch your words and speak from a place of love and care always. Never try to belittle or to outdo another, be humble and speak with authority and grace.

Whatever you do, do it to the best of your ability and with poise and dignity. Be truthful to yourself and others always. Lying will come back and bite you in the butt at some point in time. Never tell a 'white' or little lie either. Never withhold the truth, or purposefully only speak half a truth; no, rather always be open and honest in all your interactions with people.

You cannot hide your thoughts in the quantum field; they are all known and hold serious consequences for you and others.

Life will never give you more than you can handle, and if you are in dire straits, ask for help. Help is always available to you – all you have to do is ask. You will receive! This age-old law has always and will always apply, ready to assist you at anytime. You are just as important to God as the next person; every hair on your body is known to God. Nothing escapes this truth. I beg you to start knowing this truth and make it your own.

Never in a million years can there be another like you, or will there ever be another like you. You are unique and precious, a child of God, you are God. Know that there is a plan with everything in life, even if it does not make sense at the moment and life feels so overwhelming. Years down the line you might only get the answer to a past event or experience which you had. Then you will know that the event or experience was just part of learning to love yourself and the whole more. The end plan is to create a wonderfully beautiful world living in harmony with your God and all the other Gods on the planet.

Before we get to there we are constantly attracting situations and experiences into our lives by our thoughts, words and deeds. Never speak badly of another, as you are opening yourself up to the law of Karma. In turn all good words that you speak lead to good Karma and internal happiness. You create your world, and your world has an effect on the whole. You can decide whether to participate or do nothing. There's no judgment placed on you, whatever you decide to do, as you have free will to create as you see fit, bearing the consequences of your creation.

BLISS IS A NATURAL STATE ARISING FROM 'NO HUMAN-MIND'

OUR REALITY IS EVER-EXPANDING AS we move along the journey in life, and for that reason there are no wrongs and rights. That which is termed 'wrong' today might very well be 'right' tomorrow, and what is termed 'right' today might be 'wrong' tomorrow. We are in a quantum field, and the quantum field contains all known and unknown possibilities which we are here to explore and experience. We are here to learn and remember who we are - a God connected to all the other Gods and to the Mind of God. God has existed forever and will exist forever. God is nowhere and everywhere at the same time.

The paradox of nowhere and everywhere might have you in a flat panic. The thinking that God might be nowhere is a very intricate concept for our human minds to conceptualize. As with the paradox where I earlier mentioned that everything stems from nothing via our thinking. The same applies to where God is - God is everywhere via systemic growth, evolution and expansion from nowhere. The outreach of God's love is ever-present and expanding into new paradigms and dimensions, and the present moment holds within it the only important time, the now.

In this 'present moment' you start to create the next moment and contemplate the next experience to be had.

You are boundless and limitless, yet many of us have placed certain constraints and restrictions on who we are. We need to investigate these constraints and restrictions, releasing the limiting views of who we are and be that which we are, God. God does not care as much for the physical as we do, it merely chose a body in order to make known the unknown and is guided by the spirit and soul to experience and grow into a higher understanding of Itself, the self.

See your spirit as your Higher Self guiding you and your soul as the seat responsible for capturing the emotions by way of feelings associated to your experiences in life. Hence the reason why when you feel pain, suffering, depressed, disheartened, sad, lost and rejected in life you feel the emotion deep within the centre of your heart, the place where the soul is situated. The same goes for blissful feelings of exhilaration, excitement, joy, enthusiasm, love and peace. The latter are far more superior as these positive feelings are actual states of mind and have the capability to extend outwards and around your whole body for several meters, filling and expanding your auric field.

God is thought, and from thought creation and the whole universe was born, those living and not living – in spirit. Even the ones on the spiritual side of the veil are quantum and play an important role in the development and progression of all those living on the physical side of the veil. Think of it this way, in some way you are connected to spirit as nothing is not spirit, even in the physical you are partly spirit.

Your spirit and Higher Self is connected to you always and travels with you everywhere. Even in times of desperation your God is with you, giving assistance to you when you ask for help and guiding you to resolve and move forward. Be open to receiving guidance as it comes from the other side. Actually, the other side is this side. We have drawn a line between the physical and spiritual worlds and we cannot, it's impossible to do so. Start accepting the truth about *the oneness principle*: all life is quantumly connected and form part of the whole.

Your Higher Self is your eternal observer self, and there develops a vastness one can only begin to understand when you start to accept this principle and make it your own. Live like you are everything and nothing, be at one with all life and embrace duality as though there is no duality, because duality causes separation. Recognize the importance thereof in order to grow and obtain valuable knowledge and wisdom, but keep in mind that it truly does not exist.

Separation is only visible through the naked eye, the untrained human observer and mind. Once you start to look deeper and go more inward you'll see what I mean. You'll start to be filled with a sense of awe and wonder surpassing the normal states of existence known to most of humanity. There will be a rise and sense of oneness with all living elements and parts. The Masters speak so freely and joyously of oneness as the eternal love binding and holding us all together. This state of oneness brings on experiences of pure ecstasy and bliss. A feeling like no other arises as bliss transcends, and ultimately from this blissful state nirvana arises when the 'monkey-mind' finally subsides.

There is no easy way for this to transpire, and it takes extreme dedication and devotion to the cause, with an iron will to succeed and be reunited with your Higher Self. A merger takes place between the personal and impersonal selves; creating a 'Christ', a 'Buddha', a 'God-man' realized. A divine being that lives forever in the now and knows no past or future. He or she is making known the unknown, continuously creating their reality in the quantum field of the now.

Can you imagine not thinking for but one minute, how liberating it would be to give your human mind a rest? Imagine the joy that comes from resting and being at peace with a greater part of who you are. This profound wisdom is available for all, a mind that knows it is God and can manifest anything whatsoever it desires to experience from this point; including wealth, health and joy.

Fuelled by a desire to make this reality a truth for me, my journey has lead me to states of bliss and joy. The magic and wonder which I have experienced in these brief moments cannot be done justice by the written word and needs to be experienced by the individual to know for themselves. We come from the plane of bliss and we are returning there by making heaven a place on earth. Earth is the new heaven and all we need to do is to be fully present in the now.

Being fully present in the now is an interesting concept as we are always in the now. This a truth, but we have past events and future activities captivating our minds and taking us out of being truly fully present in the moment. Be wholly engaged with your every thought, word and action; know what you are constantly thinking, saying and doing. Be present in a meditative state, stay alert and let awareness guide you're every action.

Know that you are God and have a destiny to fulfil in every moment of your life, experiencing the unknown. Know you are creating in every moment of your journey and can alter any sequence of events at will, and thus change your life's path. There is no predestined outcome, only the outcome your heart and soul desire for you to experience, which is fuelled and created by your thoughts from your Higher Self.

Your focus determines your future, hence the reason why we need to be aware of what we focus on in every moment. Your every thought and action has an impact on the collective universal consciousness and draws each quantum possibility closer to you by the second.

Exercise 8 - Candle focus

Make sure there is no air movement present; then light a candle (preferably a white candle), and place it about 50cm to 1.5m in front of you, at eye level. Take your seat and make yourself comfortable, whilst making sure the flame of the candle appears at eye level in front of you. You can play some meditative music in the background if you like, to create a chilled, relaxed and peaceful atmosphere.

With this practice we are aiming to become aware of the human thinking mind; stilling this mind – 'no human–mind' or nothingness – by focusing and placing our total awareness on the blue flame in the hollow middle of the candle's wick. Just allow for the thoughts to pass through without judging any or yourself. Your human mind has been on auto-pilot for years and may take lots of practice to still. As Buddha says, 'If one sees not when steering into space, with the mind, one observes the mind, one destroys distinctions and one reaches Buddhahood!'

Very slowly the thinking of the human mind will start to dissolve and as this starts to happen, the surrounding area will begin to grey and dim somewhat, losing picture configuration and a void or tunnel zoom will begin to appear with only the candle being at your focal point. If this happens to you, know that you are on the right track. Be patient, as it may take some practice to reach this point.

You may also use this practice to create and attract your desires into your life by placing a picture of your desire (with your mind's eye) inside the blue flame's hollow, whilst gazing and focusing on it. By placing a picture of what you want to create in the hollow flame and then by focusing on this picture you are sending signals of the image into the quantum field of what you would like to create and attract into your life. Your subconscious mind or Higher Self will start to pull the energy strings in order to create this reality and make it an absolute.

There are no wrongs or rights. I use this exercise every morning mainly to still my human thinking mind. If I do this for an extended period of time, I enter into states of higher awareness, which includes joy, peace and stillness. We are endeavouring to shift our every day perceptions of reality and at the same time change the brain's neural pathways, to bring on new found joy and happiness.

THE POWER OF QUANTUM HEALING

HOW DO PEOPLE HEAL THEMSELVES from cancer and other diseases? Easy: they have direct access to the ever-present quantum field where all possibilities of health, wealth, joy and much more exist. All they have to do is access the field and change the way they think about the disease. It's that easy to do, anything can be altered and a split second is all it takes.

Since everything is mind, all cancers and other diseases of the body can be healed by shifting your thoughts. Even HIV, herpes, thrush, and for that matter any deadly disease alive today can be healed by the power of the mind. You have complete control over each and every aspect of your life and all you need to do is ask for guidance and guidance will be given.

You might say, 'but it is not that easy', and you would be correct. Changing a person's thinking is probably one of the most difficult tasks one can ever endeavour to accomplish. To change, you first have to acknowledge that you have an illness, and then ask the illness, 'what are you here to *teach me?*' Once you have the learning and understanding you can create an affirmation to heal the disease. Whether the lesson is self-love, self-worth, letting go of guilt, letting go of rejection, forgiveness, loving others more, or for whatever reason the illness exists in the body; learn the lesson and move forward with greater understanding.

Even if you manage to do this, it can be a very hard and treacherous road ahead to full recovery, and many succumb as they are unable to shift their thinking. They are unable to connect to their Higher Self as the power of the human mind overshadows their greater Higher Self. The healing is actually triggered by thinking and connecting to your quantum part or Higher Self, which accepts the healing, and your innate transfers the message to the physical body and within a flash of the eye the tumour or disease can be cured. I could describe it as an intuitive belief and knowingness that you are healed.

As I stated earlier, the body's intelligence is not run by the brain, but by your innate and Higher Self parts, as this is who you actually are, a quantum being. You need to believe you are healed, and hold that image in your mind's eye as though the healing has already taken place, or else nothing will happen. See yourself healed, walking or running with complete ease, hold the picture in your mind and do not attach any time to the outcome, just know you are healthy in this moment.

I stress the importance for you to only see and feel the healthy you, holding the picture clearly and to believe the healing has already occurred. By focusing on a healthy body and not accepting the unhealthy body as your reality you are reprogramming the brain's neural pathways and healing your physical body. You have the power to create with your mind anything and undo anything that's been created; it's only a thought away.

Healing works the same as any other part of creation, whether you are building a house and decide to change your design, planting tomatoes in your garden and later decide to plant spinach as it will grow better. All facets of healing start by changing your thinking, and mentally reprogramming the working of the brain's neural pathways; and in so doing you are changing your DNA and genetic patterning in the quantum field. The two processes are inseparable.

With the mind you are connecting to a consciousness far more superior than your physical body. You are endeavouring to connect to your Higher Self to heal the disease in the body. We continue to see plenty of miraculous healings in the world, but for most this principle remains a difficult approach to follow to accomplish health and vitality once again. Remember: God is inside you and is you!

FOLLOWING YOUR INTUITION AND GOD-THOUGHT

THERE ARE AN INFINITE NUMBER of possibilities existing in the quantum field. Just think of the mixture of different jobs in the marketplace and the diverse number of companies out there today. All originated from a thought which satisfied a need or lack coming from an individual. The lack or need gave birth to a new idea or concept being explored and pursued by the individual.

Every year there's an array of new stories being brought to life by thousands of authors. Where do all these ideas come from? It comes from our mind and our intuition, which is connected to the quantum field and Mind of God. Every piece of artwork or design comes from an infinite collection of possibilities available to us.

All of these authors believed in their idea, in themselves and the greater part of who they are. They had full belief in their ability to create a marvellously new romantic love-story or sci-fi adventure for the reader. They were open, connected and downloading information from the quantum field. Each one of us has the potential to connect and create the life and world we so desire. You must aspire to be the best 'you' whether that be an author, architect, accountant or whoever you would like to be.

All you have to do is start tuning in, and ask for guidance from the quantum field and God. Ask the questions and you will receive the answers. All things are known by God and the quantum field is what I call the 'field of dreams'. Dream bigger and brighter, get out of the human thinking mind and into God's Mind; let your intuition guide you to higher heights and grander experiences. Let synchronicity be your guide and follow the subtle thoughts that are given to you each day by your God-connection of what you should be aspiring to become.

Each person on the planet has a talent, and all you have to do is start working on yours. Start mining your 'Akashic Record'[36] for information about your unique talents by connecting more to your Higher Self. Your Akashic Record holds all the wisdom and knowledge which you have owned over all your incarnations, and thus, by mining your Akashic Record, you are pulling out learned wisdom to help you in this life.

Human beings have been interacting consciously and unconsciously with this vibrational body of energies throughout history. These interactions have been both deliberate and accidental. Virtually every major traditional religion makes reference to the Akashic Records as 'the Book of Life' and 'the Book of God's Remembrance'.[37] This body of wisdom has been an ever-present source of spiritual support for many people, religions and traditions.

Each person's Higher Self is there to assist them on the planet and to move them more into alignment by merging the physical and metaphysical aspects of their being. Do not

---

[36] The Akashic Records is a dimension of consciousness that contains a vibrational record of every soul and its journey. The record is completely available everywhere, not affected by location and time.

[37] We find various references in the Bible; see New American Standard Bible, New Testament in the book of Luke 10:20 - 'Nevertheless do not rejoice in this, that the spirits are subject to you, but rejoice that your names are recorded in heaven.'

compare yourself with other people and their talents; work on harvesting your own talents.

The more you explore your talents, the more you will develop and improve them. The world's best athletes, swimmers, golfers, actors, authors and artists all started at the bottom and worked their way to the top through effort and dedication. Their eyes were solely fixed on doing the best they could, they were inspired to perform and do better than the day before. Tune in and focus on cultivating a mind-set that seizes the best in you, for the sole reason of pursuing your own dreams.

EXPANDING YOUR AWARENESS INTO THE ONENESS OF LOVE

YOU'RE PROBABLY THINKING, 'ALL THIS is great, but I want more information on how this quantum theory works'. Earlier in the book we discussed that your DNA and genetic makeup originate from your parents, and theirs in turn from their parents, and so on. Each generation has a direct influence on the next generation, and each soul chose their life and body in order to explore and grow in awareness and consciousness.

We are learning different aspects of who we are from shame, guilt, apathy, grief, fear, desire, anger, pride, courage, neutrality, willingness, acceptance, reason, love, peace and joy. These attributes are tied to levels of consciousness that we are connected to in the quantum field. There are all multi-dimensional facets at play in the quantum field and we are continually learning to integrate and balance various aspects of these throughout our life.

I'll use the example of love; love, not just for your husband or wife, but also for your parents, your siblings, your friends, your colleagues, your neighbourhood, strangers, the shop owner, the beggar on the street, nature, animals, your country, other countries and the world. Within the energy of love we have various facets from romantic, brotherly, friendly, and neighbourly with many more aspects always at play.

Each of these elements have a frequency and vibration attached to them, and as humans we tend to express love to other humans depending on our mood and the role the individual plays in our life. These are mind-sets which we have created over time to establish a means of how we should greet and treat all humans. Each mind-set has a quantum effect placing boundaries and restrictions according to our social network of acceptable standards. There is nothing wrong with the way you choose to express your love to another, just know that you are expressing affection and love in many different ways each day.

Can you hug a stranger the same way you hug a friend or family member? Next time you go to a dinner party where you meet new people, hug each person as you would hug a very close friend. Do this with every person in the room who you meet, without differentiating with anyone. Have the intent on greeting each person as though you are greeting a dear friend. Just observe what happens. You will find that some people will back away, and others will accept your kind and loving embrace. Those who accept your embrace, not backing away, have a greater understanding of the word love. They understand that all people in the quantum field are family and have opened up to a more expansive love with fewer boundaries.

You might say, 'well that's speculative and untrue for me'. Think about it this way: would any of the Masters embrace family different? Of course not, they saw each person as family and embraced each as though they were family with the same love and affection. To them it did not matter whether you were a friend, stranger, murderer or prostitute; each and every person to them was important and no divide was placed upon that truth. Studies have been done to confirm and validate the benefits of sincerely hugging, it increases trust and morality as the feel-good hormone oxytocin gets released by the brains neurotransmitters.[38]

All I am saying is to treat each person with the same love and respect and do not let your ego and personality get in the way. Do not change the way you act in front of different people, it's all about alignment of your true self and nature. Although the above applies, I am aware that we are living in a world and society with a mix of different cultures and views, each with their own and special way of conduct.

Why do we constrict our love from flowing freely? We have built walls around ourselves to protect us from hurt as we do not fully understand the real essence of love and how it relates to our world. We place boundaries and restrictions on love and in so doing we are containing a greater element of ourselves. Every time we expand our view we expand quantumly, affecting the whole. Nothing goes unnoticed in the quantum field as we expand and integrate our understanding. Every time we do this we are recalibrating our view and perspective of love in its entirety.

We are ever-expanding all attributions of who we are; such as magnificence, greatness, honour, respect, humility, humbleness, strength, power, love, sincerity, joy, abundance, success, gratitude and many more facets and dimensions of who we are. Still, we do not understand that everything in essence is love. We have to work on all elements and features of love to understand who we really are. Each element and feature makes up various degrees in the quantum field, with each individual deciding what their truth is.

---

[38] Studies done by Paul J. Zak on the benefits of sincere hugging that lasts for 20 seconds, shows that we release the hormone oxytocin from the brain, increasing trust, morality, safety, mental and physical health. Website: www.moralmolecule.com

We all have a different view of love and how it should feel and even look like. We base all our observations and interactions of love on such a small perspective. Love is the water flowing down the river, love is the lion killing her prey, love is the birds singing in the morning, love is giving the beggar food or not; nothing escapes love as it encompasses all facets of life and is life. Love is oneness as it encapsulates everything.

A RECALIBRATING OF SELF LEADS TO AN INDIRECT RECALIBRATING OF THE WHOLE

WHEN YOU LET GO OF any restricting views previously held by the mind and open up to a greater expansiveness and awareness, you recalibrate your human mind and Higher Self. What's even more fantastic is that when you grow and change your relationship with love you give permission for the same to transpire in your parents, your family and in the whole world. With each new found perspective and view of love you change, recalibrate and align in the quantum field.

A recalibration of self leads to an indirect recalibration of the whole. You start to see that your parents did the best they knew how with the teachings and lessons received from their parents, and their parents from their parents. You stop blaming them for not loving you enough, for not always being there for you, for being a bad parenting example by smoking and drinking too much or for using drugs. You forgive them and move on, you break the negative patterns of belief which existed and start to create your own destiny. You release them in the quantum field and love them for the lessons they brought your way.

You and you alone can break the old pattern of beliefs existing in your family and within your DNA. You have the ability to amend anything in the quantum field, even to the point of altering your very genetic makeup. One of your parents might be suffering from a chronic condition, for example blood pressure, cancer, diabetes or cholesterol; but these need not be carried forward by you. You can alter any predisposed genetic condition by connecting to your Higher Self even to the point of slowing down and stopping your aging process.

You do not have to accept the 'sins' of the fathers and mothers as your own. All you need to do is to start speaking to your Higher Self, the quantum part of you and ask for guidance on how to break the chains binding generations together. You do not have to accept the same destiny as your parents, we are here to rewrite our past and create 'magic' (reality) along the way. There are people that can shift their mind's thinking overnight, creating new neural pathways in the brain, and thus a new reality unfolds; but for most this takes practice to focus on the already healed body and mind.

The key, as with everything, is to visualize a healed and healthy body running or walking without any discomfort. See it as your reality, feel it as your reality. How would you feel running or walking with ease? Go into the feeling of being grateful and joyous. Life is a gift and by the act of gratitude you evoke a universal force surpassing human comprehension.

How do you think Jesus healed the people in the Bible? He did not heal them; they healed themselves by recognizing the God in him, and by accepting the healing from him they allowed themselves to be healed. They had complete belief and trust that he could heal them, but in actual fact they were responsible for their own healing. They were all healed quantumly by their own thinking and Higher Self. Jesus in essence was the catalyst and mirror to what was possible for them.

See yourself always being able to recalibrate any behaviour, attitude, belief or view preciously held upon which you base your life. Everything can be changed within an instant via the quantum field, a field always present and ready for a new experience to unfold. Miraculous healings have and can take place overnight. A new job opportunity can arise, a new book can make its way to the foreground, a new way of communicating can be established, a new energy source can be discovered; all thoughts and ideas come from this field.

With each recalibration of self we are recalibrating our past and our future. By expanding our view of love we are in essence recalibrating the collective consciousness of the whole, as everything is interlinked via the quantum field.

Exercise 9 - Gratitude

Giving thanks and being appreciative is in my view one of the most important daily habits one must cultivate for oneself. Every day you should focus on feeling gratitude in your heart, as this is one of the four main pillars which form part of meditation and prayer. The other three pillars of meditation are: first, to think of nothing – 'no human-mind'; secondly to connect with all life and your surroundings – expansiveness; and thirdly to concentrate and focus in order to create the world and reality you desire.

By being thankful for the blessings in life, such as being healthy, having a job, having food on a table, a roof over your head and warm bed to sleep in, you are sending powerful signals of energy into the quantum field and the ripples will return to you twofold as gratitude relates to the law of cause and effect, and to the law of attraction.

The size and scale of thanks does not matter as it is all about the act of feeling heartfelt gratitude and love for your blessings. Expressing gratitude and thanks can be done at anytime of the day, seeing the sunrise or sunset, smelling a flower, receiving a hug from a dear friend and being appreciative.

Make yourself a gratitude list; it does not have to be longwinded, just a small list of appreciation. Every morning take some time to focus on feeling gratitude for each entry on your list. To God, the sincere expression of being thankful is much more important than the quantity. Gratitude is an act of love, intertwined as love in the highest form.

IF YOU ARE STILL ALIVE, YOUR MISSION IN LIFE IS NOT YET COMPLETED

SEE THE QUANTUM FIELD AS an allowance to change for the better or worse - the choice is yours. Freewill is yours, you choose, but know your every choice will have consequences. These consequences will be your responsibility to deal with, whether you label them as good or bad. We are here to explore the scale of infinity in the universe which leads to oneness.

We have hardly lived, each one of us have so many beliefs and barriers holding us back due to our perception of how we should live or of what we should be doing. We get tied up in the human mind, over-thinking and analyzing; we get stuck in a rut. We give away our power to create, and the human logic keeps us trapped like there's no tomorrow. We are forever planning ahead and not being present in the moment.

So much joy can be found by living fully in each moment of life. All of life has to do with your attitude and how you are applying it. Even changing a tire after driving over a nail in the road can give you joy. The joy lies in the experience and being present with each new incident. This experience can gift you with new wisdom and knowledge - you fixing and being able to change your own tire. Can you say, 'I own this wisdom'? If you have not changed a tire, how will you know how it felt like to accomplish this task? Yes, you heard me correctly; this, too, is a minor victory along the journey of life.

The smallest and seemingly insignificant event can bring either great joy or frustration; this depends on how you view the situation, as does everything in life. Your attitude and will to experience will catapult you towards new and adventurous times if you are open to life. Allow for the journey to guide you, being willed by exuberance and joy. The universe and quantum field will see that you are open and eager to experience more of life.

All of life is experience, and only through your eyes do you have the choice to see each event as frustrating, or as a blessing in disguise. Never focus on the negative, always allow for the positive side. Be open and able to see both sides of the coin. Duality is twofold, in fact, every experience is twofold; your eyes and mind decide whether you see it as positive or negative. You must enjoy the ride, and laugh and have fun along the way.

Are you able to see the bigger picture? Just think what might have happened if your tire had eluded the nail. The incident could have helped you miss a serious car accident in which you could have lost your life. For all purposes you were destined to die on that day; but, because God and your soul decided the time was not yet right, the universe and quantum field arranged for a puncture. Always be aware of a higher power ever-present and guiding you along the journey. Some people may say their guardian angel was protecting and leading them towards their highest good. Your guardian angel is in fact your Higher Self which is connected to the Higher Selves of all the other Gods.

You are always at the right place at right time, even in death or in an accident, as nothing happens by chance. There are no random events or occurrences, all are synchronistically arranged by your Higher Self and God. You cannot escape anything along the road which has been ordained to occur. You can, however, alter your view and belief of reality, which causes a ripple effect and change in the quantum field, altering your timeline and destiny.

This will change your life's path and you might head into another direction altogether, the choice is always yours. If you had stayed on the same path you might have collided with a truck and ended up dead. You, your Higher Self by the power of your own freewill, decided to alter your point of entry back to the spirit world and in doing so a new life path has unfolded with new possibilities and experiences ready and waiting.

If you are still alive, it means your mission in life is not yet complete. Go and create remarkable new experiences!

EACH SOUL HAS A UNIQUE AGENDA IN LIFE

PRIOR TO YOU ENTERING THERE are certain events that the soul has requested to experience in order to learn from and gain a new understanding and wisdom. Hence the reason for choosing your body, your family, your surroundings, your upbringing and even your country of birth. You have entered the physical world and placed yourself at the precise spot where you have chosen to learn the most in this lifetime.

In stating the above, there are also souls who have entered to experience a chilled and relaxed lifetime, supporting other souls whilst they are doing the hard work and graft. This time around they may take it easy as the previous lifetime or two could have been very challenging and demanding. Every soul has a different agenda which can be altered by the soul at any time.

I stated earlier, that some souls come in with the knowledge that they are going to die at a very early age and this will either cause their parents to grow stronger in their love for each other, or cause them split up because the pain was too unbearable to handle. They could not bear to be with their spouse any longer as they were a constant reminder of the sadness, emotional hurt and pain felt from losing a child. Tragedies have the ability to rip people apart or pull them together - be wise and choose the latter.

Maybe this very same husband and wife decide to move forward in love by leaving all sadness and sorrow behind. When they do, they may be gifted with a beautiful new baby to love. Their love for each other will now be stronger and more endearing. They have learned the lesson of gratitude and being thankful for each blessing in life. I know this is certainly not always the case, and more often than not couples will only have each other, and that too is good enough. It is all a part of God's divine and loving plan.

THE IMPORTANCE OF ACTIVATING THE BRAIN'S DORMANT NEURAL PATHWAYS

OUR PLANET AND HUMANITY HAVE been rocked by numerous natural disasters, horrific events and wars over the past century alone. There have been two world wars, a cold war, and wars in the Middle East; in fact most continents and countries have been rocked by war. You name it, there has been a war, war between brothers, war between nations, war between races, and the list just keeps getting longer and longer. And for what reason? War is always because of a difference in opinion.

What happens is that, we hold onto our view so strongly that we cannot see the bigger picture. We are so narrow-minded and closed in our view to suit our belief as we are scared to believe in anything else. We stand by our truth, not budging an inch. We cannot shift; we believe our truth and will die for our cause. How silly and foolish; we think we are always right and stay fixed, cast in stone in our righteousness.

Start to broaden your horizon, look and see with new eyes. Be present, be conscious, and be aware of what you are thinking, doing and saying. See and be aware of what are you attracting into your quantum field. Question your beliefs; have an open mind to change any belief when you feel it does not sit well with your soul any longer. Be happy to find a new truth, as there are many more to discover along your journey.

Trust in the process of life, as it never brings you more than you can handle. Connect to your soul, feed your soul, and your life will shine and you will be an example to many. Live like a king, but be humble as a beggar. Recalibration of self takes place every moment in the quantum field. This field recalibrates trillions upon trillions of aspects of who you think you are. The energy particles are reformulated, modified and adapted according to the view of your Higher Self.

Scientists say we use less than ten percent of our brain, so what do you think the other ninety percent of the brain is for? We need to activate this large and dormant piece of grey matter, every neural pathway has to fire, and then we become a 'Christ' or 'Buddha'. They live in the now with complete control over their bodies, with the ability to manifest food and water at leisure. This can only take place once we are able to let go of the 'monkey-mind' as this mind no longer rules our life and destiny.

We have to recalibrate and recalibrate over and over until we finally reach a point in time of becoming a 'God-man' realized. In this state we are not driven by our egos, lack of any kind or self-worth issues; we know who we are, we are God living as a man. We have transcended the paradoxes and no longer have any need for them as our domain is the infinite oneness.

With each shift and recalibration of the self we become closer to our Higher Self, with our glorious magnificence shining through on the one end of the tunnel, and on the other end our presence and essence of pure humbleness. The opposites collide, reuniting with true greatness and grace; and in the process leaving ego, power and brute strength behind.

THE IMPORTANCE OF INCREASING YOUR LIGHT SPECTRUM

THERE IS A GRAND PLAN for each one of us, but the plan is not always known. Consider where you were and what you were doing five or even ten years ago. Could you have guessed how life would have unfolded? No, you could not! That's the main purpose to life – to make known the unknown, which can only be done through experiences that ultimately lead to wisdom and knowledge.

How do you experience? You can only experience in the now; not the past and not the future. You need to live each moment as if it is your last. You do not know what tomorrow will bring – a car accident, being diagnosed with cancer or losing a loved one. Stay present, live like you have no tomorrow and love with all of your heart. Be kind and sincere in all your actions and always see the good in other humans.

Have peace in the quantum field and system, as it's far grander than you can even begin to imagine with your human mind. Know that you are a microcosm of the macrocosm; life within life, the infinity spiral progressing, forever changing in the eternity of now.

With each recalibration and shift, you help the planet and earth to shift with you. We are intertwined in the matrix of energy, and energy is all there is. As you begin to release and stop to feed your anger, envy, jealousy, sorrow, regret, greed, arrogance, self-pity, guilt, resentment, inferiority, lies, false pride, superiority and ego, you start to free yourself from the 'evil' mind. You move into a place where only good enters, and start to see with new eyes.

You start to see everything as good; and only joy, peace, love, hope, serenity, humility, kindness, benevolence, empathy, generosity, truth, compassion and faith can enter your heart and 'good' mind. As you start to see with new eyes you realize everything has a place and is just the way it is supposed to be. You can smile, laugh and cry at the same time, as this new found knowledge and joy enters your soul.

In the process of recalibration and changing into a new way of understanding life, the quantum field and all connections can be extremely lonely and unpleasant at times, and all you might want to do is crawl away and die. Know that when you have completed your soul's recalibration and are moving through the dark times, the light always awaits you on the other side. The light is always present, even in times of solitude your God travels with you.

The journey leads us towards letting go of the ego, and to moving more into the God part of who you are. The ego dies hard; it wants to survive and fester in the human mind, the analytical thinking mind, and wants to reason its way back into your life. This is the push and pull of light and dark energies that is the way of the system of duality. The ultimate goal is to let go of the dark energy with your new found wisdom and knowledge gathered from life's experiences, and to move into the light.

We are explorers, navigating a structure built out of energy; a celestial spectrum of light. With the shift of each belief or view we open the door for more light in the form of love to enter, expanding our consciousness. With new wisdom and knowledge comes a greater array of light, a knowingness we did not possess before. With each step we become lighter, as our spiritual light body expands by letting go of the dark.

There is no timeframe, and with each recalibration along the way we are shedding parts of who we are not, and accepting more of who we are. Our God walks with us and guides us to the next step along this journey. Remember what I said, the journey for each person is different and totally unique, custom-made for them, by them. That's the beauty of life – as each progression fills your God with more love and light.

With each recalibration you expand your spiritual body, a body consisting of an enormously vast spectrum of light. This light spectrum is called the love of God, an infinite number of light rays filling your spiritual body; all building blocks of compassion and love to glorify the magnificence of your Higher Self. These are all elements at play in the quantum field. See yourself as going back up the spectrum of light to reunite with your Higher Self, guided by the Mind of God.

THE JOURNEY TO ENLIGHTENMENT AND BECOMING FULLY QUANTUM

GOD KNOWS NO TIME, SO even a newly wedded couple wanting kids may have to surrender their need. The baby may only enter two or three years down the line, because there are certain life lessons the parents are required to learn before the baby can enter the physical world. The couple may need to increase their frequency and vibration by defining for themselves a new set of beliefs, views and values. As the result of their increase in love and truth, the parents are now able to fall pregnant with a little one.

Maybe the parents were first required to obtain a higher consciousness and energy in order for the baby to enter. Divine timing created a new reality and gave allowance for the baby as a being of higher consciousness to enter. Patience and new found wisdom obtained by the parents allowed for the act to come about. You do not own the timelines and there might be a range of life lessons vital to the parents' growth before the baby can enter the physical domain.

Even enlightenment is not for you to know, you just need to do the best you can with what you know. Enlightenment is an allowance that can only take place once the being has integrated an enormously wide range of beliefs and views, after which there arises a new found understanding within them. This is a merger between the human and God parts of who you are. A meld has formed making you fully quantum and able to do anything your Higher Self desires to do.

There is an integration of the linear into quantum energy, leading to enlightenment. This requires your being to open up to chaos and an unstructured way of doing. Quantum has nothing to do with being intellectual, analytical, logical or comparing. You need to cast all of these overboard as they do not exist in a quantum world, the human mind cannot go there. We cannot compartmentalize quantum beings as they are without human structure as we know God is. God is all things, always and at all times. There is no linear design structure available that can hold Source as it is the Creator of all.

These things cannot be reasoned or even tried to be explained by the human mind, it has no quantum comprehension. The intellect and reason cannot take you there as it's connected to the part of the brain that keeps you enslaved in three and four dimensions, your survival mind. You are far more than you appear to be, you are a spiritual being with the Creator's power and strength resting inside of you. The unconditional love of God is ever-present as we are peeling the layers of the onion to get to our core.

Enlightenment is a state of 'no human–mind' that arises spontaneously when thinking finally subsides. In this state you accept everyone for who they are; their views, beliefs and journey. You understand that all people are exactly where they are supposed to be, and so are you. You have journeyed to the centre of your own soul and back and have found your truth in love.

You are the truth, the light and the love of God. You understand the principle of: *God the Father (Mother), God the Son (Daughter) and the Holy Spirit; as they are in truth equivalent to; 'the*

Mind of God', 'your Higher Self' and 'the Quantum Field'. You let go of duality and non-duality brings forth a new understanding to the dimensions of love and life. You know that you are everything and nothing at the same time. You are free to dream and create for all eternity, forever present in the now.

Quantum beings have no concept of time, and one day or a thousand years have the same meaning to them, as time to them does not exist. They live in a forever young and healthy body, moving through life and the universe, enjoying experience after experience. Our human minds are what hold us back from being fully quantum. Once you let go of your ego and allow for the observer self or Higher Self to take over your life will be transformed into a beautiful flower, blossoming for all to see.

That is why Jesus could proclaim; 'Believe Me that I am in the Father and the Father is in Me; otherwise believe because of the works themselves. Truly, truly, I say to you, he who believes in Me, the works that I do, he will do also; and greater works than these he will do; because I go to the Father. Whatever you ask in My name, that will I do, so that the Father may be glorified in the Son.'[39]

The real truth behind Jesus' words are that, he, 'the Son', has merged into oneness with God - the Father and the Holy Spirit; and by doing so he was able to perform that which we term 'miracles' in the name of the Father, the Son and the Holy Spirit. He further more advocates that any man or woman are able to do the same works, and some may even do greater works than he has done, so that the Father (Mother) may be glorified through the Son and Daughter.

Don't you think it's interesting to hear that Jesus himself refers to these so called 'miracles' as mere *works*? Jesus never

---

[39] New American Standard Bible, New Testament in the book of John 14:11-13.

called them 'miracles', because he knew they were inspirational pieces of art preformed by him, as are all things in life. All works are creative thoughts which we receive from the divine Mind of God, and have the potential to be manifested into the physical dimension. Everything you have in your life is as a result of a thought which you pursued and later manifested into the physical reality.

There are endless inspirational avenues available and ready to be explored, for example; in music, we can be a singer, song writer, composer, belong to a band, play an instrument, focus on a genre of choice, be a band manager, work behind the scenes on the production set, and the list just continues for this one element of life. Just think of the scope and potential out there today, the various avenues of business, farming, leisure, but to name a few.

Why do you think Jesus said that we need to become like a child to enter the Kingdom of heaven?[40] Children show unconditional love and affection, their minds have not been contaminated with any kind of judgment, analyzing or comparing. Children are explorers and seek to learn through experience, not labelling anything as good or bad, wrong or right. They only seek to live the moment by finding the highest pleasure in each second, as they have no bearing of time. They love without any boundaries or constraints and trust wholeheartedly.

We, as adults, are the brain-washers, the ones who tell them about black and white, rich and poor and what is wrong and right for us. They are none the wiser, completely innocent, but we prescribe and indoctrinate them with how they should love,

---

[40] New American Standard Bible, New Testament in the book of Matthew 18:3 - and said, 'Truly I say to you, unless you are converted and become like children, you will not enter the kingdom of heaven.'

act and feel, based upon our perspective and learning's. They are always fully present in the now, and when they get hurt, they cry, and within a few minutes forget about ever being injured. Their minds have no concept of time and the future and they do not stay stuck in the past by holding onto grudges. They only live in the now!

START BUILDING YOUR QUANTUM BRIDGE TO SOLIDIFY YOUR GOD-CONNECTION

CLAIRVOYANTS, MEDICAL INTUITIVES, HEALERS AND kinesiologists all use the quantum field to give you a reading, and to pick up if there are any imbalances in your aura or quantum being. How is it then that the brain does not know you are developing a cancer or any other disease in the body? The brain can only pick up the disease at a later stage, only once there is pain present in the body. The reason is that the body is not governed by the brain, but by the innate and your Higher Self.

We are disconnected from our God part and an element of our journey is to build the quantum bridge, and solidify our connection to that which we are, God. Daily meditation, focusing, and working on the self will help you to build the bridge with your Higher Self. Yes, you heard me right; we are building a bridge to connect and integrate the oneness with our Higher Self.

This is a God who is not linear thinking, or debating and analyzing everything. We must let go of our human and survival mind's need to understand things before we have had the experience. The key is to let go of our human mind and meld with our Higher Self. By doing this we become one with life and are guided by our intuition and synchronicity every step along the journey. This can take many hours and years of practice – and in some instances even a lifetime to perfect as the old energy dies hard and wants to hold onto old belief patterns and views.

Our rational thinking mind cannot go to God; we can only go there with the irrational and unstructured mind, the part which connects all living organisms on the planet. This sounds crazy and totally ludicrous, but it is true; a mind with no limits is a mind totally free to explore the vastness of the cosmos. Therein lies the secret, you cannot reason yourself there as you *are* there; you just need to accept the truth. The connection between the Higher Self and God–Mind will take you anywhere and everywhere you want to go.

We required the logical, analytical and intellectual mind in order to survive in three and four dimensions; and where we are headed, the human mind must be left behind. We need to activate the Higher Self, the irrational and unstructured part, and let spiritual logic and intuition from the Mind of God be our guide. There is so much more to experience than four dimensions, and we are journeymen and women on a voyage to discover the higher planes of existence.

These higher planes have higher vibrations and frequencies, and hold for us much more joy and excitement. It involves moving out of the human 'judgmental and comparing mind', and into the acceptance of life in all its majestic glory. We are guided toward a fulfilment and realization that suffering is only due to our own lack of understanding. We transcend duality as we now have the understanding of life, it being but a marvellous illusion we created in order to discover who we truly are.

Meditation, prayer and other spiritual practices, in the case of deep breathing and yoga, are there to assist us with opening and activating our brain's pineal gland (please refer to Picture 2 - The Brain). The pineal gland is our connection to the quantum field, to our Higher Self and to the Mind of God, and from where we receive our spiritual and intuitive guidance. Our left brain is the seat of all our judgments; and by being 'the observer self', we start to surrender and dissolve all judgments that we hold.

Gradually, as we let go of duality by re-programming our brain's neural pathways, we start to awaken and enter into higher states of awareness and consciousness. During the bridge building process and changing of our brain's neural pathways, there is a slow and conscious unification between the left and the right hemispheres of the brain; as we work towards our mystical awakening and enlightenment. The part of the brain where the pineal gland is situated is directly linked and depicted in ancient teachings, mystics and different religions as the 'All-Seeing Eye of God'.[41]

If you have seen a natural healer, clairvoyant, kinesiologist or any alternative medicine practitioner, you will know that they connect to the quantum part of you, your Higher Self. How else would they know about your past and current life situations, medical and other difficulties? These elements are all connected in the quantum field, as there is no other logical way for them to be familiar with information about you and your life. They connect to your Akashic record in the quantum field, the part which knows everything about you, your innate and Higher Self.

---

[41] In Christianity called the Eye of Providence: http://en.wikipedia.org/wiki/Eye_of_Providence, in Ancient Egyptian mythology called the Eye of Horus: http://en.wikipedia.org/wiki/Eye_of_Horus and in Hinduism and Buddhism called the Third eye or Buddha Eyes: http://en.wikipedia.org/wiki/Third_eye

Kinesiology is muscle testing with the principle of asking 'yes' and 'no' questions to the individual. The individual's body and muscles will respond by either weakening or staying strong. The body has an innate, inborn intelligence which knows what is wrong or out of balance. The kinesiology practitioner will muscle test for ailments, bodily diseases or imbalances. They connect to the quantum field and the Higher Self part of the patient.

The innate is incapable of lying and always cooperates by either showing a false or true result. The body can display ailments related to mental, emotional or physical wellbeing. The practitioner will endeavour to find and correct the underlying cause of the disease, rather than simply treating or suppressing the symptoms. In doing so the practitioner can prescribe and generate a course of action to return the body to balance.

Another easy way and fairly simple method that you can use to ask the body questions is to venture down to your local esoteric shop and purchase a pendulum. If you do not have an esoteric shop nearby, be creative and make one. All you need is a piece of string and a stone or steady object. Tie the stone or steady object to one end of the string. At the opposite end, tie a knot for holding the pendulum.

A pendulum works in pretty much the same way as kinesiology, by using the quantum field to receive the answers to your questions. You first need to establish the pendulum's 'yes' and 'no' swings. This can be done by asking a 'yes' and a 'no' question known to you whilst holding the pendulum still and observing the direction of the swing and in so doing establishing the 'yes' and 'no' swinging patterns. The pendulum can only respond to 'yes' and 'no' questions and the user should only ask 'yes' and 'no' questions. By following this method you can ask and find out anything you wish to know.

Fire walking is a practice of shutting down the human logic and transcending normal barriers and beliefs held by the brain and the human mind. The part of the brain that relates to the duality of hot and cold is temporarily suspended, and the individual is able to walk over burning hot coals without feeling any discomfort or pain. This is an experience which is achievable for any person on the street after a little focus, some inspirational coaching and preparation.

THE IMPORTANCE OF MEDITATION AND PRAYER TO CONNECT TO GOD

WHY IS MEDITATION AND PRAYER so important? Meditation and prayer helps to establish the connection between all your parts connected to God. You are speaking and aiming to connect to the part of you who is far grander than your physical image. You are aspiring to connect to your Higher Self, the quantum part of you. We ask questions and expect the answers to be in our language, yet the quantum systems do not always work in this manner. You can receive intuitive flashes of thought, feelings, symbols or pictures.

Each person can tune in to listen, but we do not know what to listen for. Earlier I mentioned we are building the bridge to connect to our Higher Self and God-Mind. This connection enables us to use synchronicity by receiving clear signals, via our intuition, regarding questions or aspects we want clarity about. We are activating the antenna towers and enabling them to receive messages and signals, much like existing cellular phone and television towers.

As we become more quantum our receivers start to function better, and the messages will become clearer of what our God wants to experience and where we are supposed to go to have the next experience in life. Messages are constantly being sent out by the quantum field and all we have to do is tune in and listen. We have lost, or let me rather say forgotten, our God-connection and are busy building a bridge using meditation, prayer and other mindful practices.

Over time we will even be able to project mental images to another person or be able to telepathically communicate with friends. This, however, will still take some time before the majority of individuals are able to acquire these and other skills. Just know there are no limits. The limits are the human mind; everything is possible for the Higher Self and the key is to unify our Higher Self with the God-Mind.

During the bridge building process our human minds are still active until the final brick is laid and our Higher Self takes full control of the reins. The process and activation of our Higher Self can take years of practice and with every shift of the self and view of our world we move slowly closer, until we finally transcend duality and become one with our Higher Self. When the human thinking mind finally subsides we are completely connected to our Higher Self and follow the intuitive thoughts of creation we receive from the Mind of God.

Have you ever had the experience where you thought of someone you had not seen or spoken to in some time and shortly afterwards the person contacted you? I am sure you have, and this is just another example highlighting the power of the quantum field and the interconnectedness of all life. Each person on the planet has an important role to play in shifting their awareness to create a higher collective consciousness.

Picture 2 – The Brain

Pineal Gland

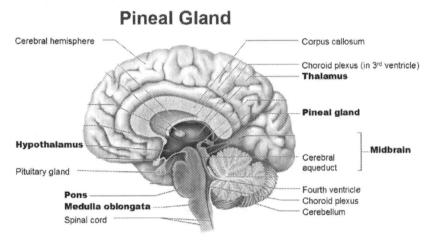

Cerebral hemisphere

Corpus callosum

Choroid plexus (in 3rd ventricle)
Thalamus

Pineal gland

Hypothalamus

Midbrain

Pituitary gland

Cerebral
aqueduct

Pons

Fourth ventricle

Medulla oblongata

Choroid plexus

Spinal cord

Cerebellum

Source reference: www.uniteunderfreedom.com/?p=2225

NAVIGATING THE
QUANTUM PUZZLE

HOW SHOULD I MEDITATE OR pray? We want to establish a connection between ourselves and God. God is us, so in essence we are talking to and asking for help and guidance on troublesome issues from ourselves. Therefore we need to be receptive to all the signs, feelings, pictures and symbols being received via our intuition. For this reason, one element of meditation and prayer relates to stillness and awareness, to be able to hear and see the flashes of intuitive thought passing through our mind.

The more you practice awareness of thought the more conscious you will become of irregular thought patterns, symbols or pictures entering your mind or of feelings in the body. Divine guidance is but a thought and question away, we just need to open ourselves up in order to receive the answers. Spirit is not linear and uses various methods of communication to send us the answers.

Constant awareness of thoughts which come to mind must be practiced at all times by one who endeavours to successfully navigate the quantum system. By our listening and seeing our thoughts, we are opening the doorway to the magic of synchronicity. Trusting our intuition and sixth sense is vitally important along the journey of spiritual guidance, and all answers are a mere question away. Answers might even come in the form of chills or goose bumps down the spine or whole body.

You need to be attentive, open to listen and receive the answers. People you meet or come across might be there to assist you with answers to your questions, or help you to heal, shift or move forward. There are no set rules, and all methods will be unique for each due to their own understanding of spirit. The quantum field is not bound by human logic and understanding, there is a higher awareness at play. Be open, be aware and listen to see the signs around you and ultimately have fun navigating the quantum puzzle.

SOCIAL MEDIA AND TECHNOLOGY HIGHLIGHTS THE UNIVERSAL CONNECTION

IN THE PAST TWO DECADES the globe entered a new area of connectivity via cellular devices, the internet and social media such as Skype, Facebook, Twitter, YouTube, Instagram, and many other similar programs. Numerous methods of communication are available in an instant via radio network signals being broadcasted over different frequencies to each other. Instant connection and access to a variety of choices lay at the fingertips of the user, whether by means of texting, phoning or browsing the World Wide Web.

It does not matter where in the world you find yourself today; you are able to instantly connect to other humans in other parts of the globe. Connectivity is available for the user at his or her leisure and convenience; they can tune in at any time at any place, ever-present. Facebook is the world's largest social media network, with an audience and membership base exceeding one billion registered users.[42] This highlights *the oneness principle* and collective consciousness that binds us all together with no discrimination of social status, race, gender or colour. Everyone can use a range of different social media to communicate to friends and family across the globe at the push of a button.

---

[42] Facebook: http://en.wikipedia.org/wiki/Facebook

THE POWERFUL HEALING VIBRATIONS OF SOUND

SOUND HAS MANY HEALING QUALITIES, and the ancients used drums and other musical instruments to evoke a stimulus which helped with altering the energy and vibration of individuals. Many ceremonies were practiced whereby uplifting the tribe and altering their consciousness was initiated by evoking a trance-like state in order to connect to the ancestors and passed loved ones. They called on the spirit world to help with rain, healing and other therapies.

It is fantastic how more and more humans are re-discovering and placing greater value on these and other ancient techniques and disciplines. Music through sound has a vibratory frequency that can alter the state by shifting the awareness of the listener and fast-tracking the connection to the Higher Self.

There are musical sounds which uplift our environment and surroundings; whereas some sounds have a negative vibratory effect. Some studies have found that violent, sexist rap and heavy metal music has a negative effect on the environment's vibration and frequency; whereas classical, classical rock, reggae, most country and pop music produce a positive influence.[43] All

---

[43] See the book, Power vs. Force written by Dr David R. Hawkins, website: www.veritaspub.com and studies done on water by Doctor Masaru Emoto, website: www.masaru-emoto.net/english/water-crystal.html

sounds have a vibratory frequency, generating and sending out energy into the quantum field affecting the consciousness of the whole.

When is the last time you listened to Bach, Beethoven or Mozart? Classical music has profound healing power and uplifting abilities, transporting the listener to higher dimensions of consciousness. Most trance or party music possess the same ability to uplift hundreds, even thousands of humans to a higher, more peaceful and loving state of living. Both touch the hearts of listeners inducing feelings of ecstasy, joy and bliss with deep feelings of love and compassion.

Music as a healing power transcends normal and traditional barriers and beliefs. Music can create unity between cultures and has the ability to connect people, places, times and events. Union and oneness songs are being played where different nations and cultures dance to the same music. Human beings love music, each tone unique with a special sound and vibration, bringing life to the world and those listening.

We as the human population are so very fortunate to be able to listen to such a wide variety of music today. More and more songs are being produced and brought to life. Each song has a life and tells a story to the listener; pure art in the making every time, inspiration from the other side of the veil. Our minds are being transported to that 'never–never' world, one note at a time. How much more magical can it be?

Can you feel the chills running down your spine? Can you fall in love with an artist and give thanks to our God for bringing us all such blessings? I absolutely love music and can listen to almost any genre, my mood determining my preference. Give yourself the gift of music and love each moment like never before. Music can only be listened to in the moment. I challenge you to go and play your favourite song and engage fully by staying present, listening and feeling the vibrations of each note penetrating your being as though you wrote the lyrics.

Use music to meditate, use music to dance, use music to play, use music to cry, use music to celebrate and use music for absolutely any occasion. You are in the driver's seat and can select a song for each occasion, making it a special experience. The magic and quantum effect via vibrations can be felt all over the planet.

Music makes an ordinary movie an epic adventure from start to finish. Music delivers the scintillating ingredient and sparks the fire in hearts of millions watching. Music captures the majestic moment and fills the soul of the movie-goer with raw emotion. Thank you God for such a beautiful gift of love.

LIVE TO EXPERIENCE THE WONDER OF LIFE'S INFINITE POSSIBILITIES

HAVE YOU EVER WATCHED AN artist in motion? A painter stroking his or her brush over a blank canvas, being totally engulfed and infused with raw inspiration in the moment? Slowly, with every stroke of the brush he or she is creating a masterpiece to be proud of. They are in the now; they only see the now and grasp the now with their full presence and being of mind. Nothing exists around them; they are fully submerged in creating a work of art.

This is how we should live each second of the day, being fully present in the now, and the now forever changing as we are walking and moving through life, one step at a time. Nothing else exists but the moment; in the moment the past holds no bearing and the future is being lived in the now. This is the principle of quantum magic as we create and we move through life.

Too many of us plan for weeks scheduling a holiday or event and in the meantime we forget to live. We are so looking forward to the holiday that our mind keeps playing pictures and we are envisioning what our holiday will be like. Then there are those people who after enjoying a memorable holiday want to relive the experience over and over and so they create movies, frequently revisiting the past experiences instead of enjoying new experiences. We have forgotten that the journey is, in a large part, about making known the unknown.

The key to the most enchanting holiday ever, is to liberate your mind beforehand from any expectations. Leave room for surprises to occur along the way, be open to adapt and change your course at any time you feel the need to do so. Surrender your need for control, being rigid and inflexible; it's during these times of no control when you will feel more alive than ever before. Live in the moment, the now, and take pleasure in exploring new concepts and ideas. Be open and allow change to find you, become part of a life that guides you to new heights.

When you follow these principles and make them a part of your reality and consciousness the most beautiful and unexpected events will start to occur. Let go of your routine by loving and embracing the fact that you do not always know your next step. Just think if you did, what would there be to look forward to experience?

Open up for new adventures, start painting your own canvas, attend some pottery or cooking classes, go on a trekking or canoeing expedition, be spontaneous and dare to live. Let your imagination expand to the ends of the earth, connecting to that glorious energy field by finding new inspiration. The quantum field has an infinite array of ideas and possibilities. Focus on nothingness and have your God part connect to the field by pulling a new idea out of the sky.

Live to experience the new, wild and untamed, make the rules and set the boundaries; you are the painter, with each stroke shaping your life. Move with grace and ease, and allow for the wonder of the moment to find you. For me this has been my dream to live life as God and make known the unknown, to create in the moment as I journey and explore all avenues unknown to me.

FREE YOUR MIND FROM PAST EXPERIENCES AND LIVE IN THE NOW

THIS BRINGS US TO OTHER important questions. So why do I not get my heart's desire within a second or moment? Why is it so difficult to manifest a fabulous new job or car? The main reason is that you either have energy stuck in the past or in the future and you are not living in the now or you are not holding your vision clear enough in your mind's eye. Your God needs to believe without a doubt that the job is already there, or the car is already an existing reality in your world.

The Masters are able to create anything within a split second as they have all their energy available in the now to create their desire and reality. They have no energy stuck in the past or in the future as they live in the now. The Higher Self is your tool for creation, but at this stage it is being navigated by a minion. The minion needs to know he or she is God, and when the day arrives you will be able to construct your new car within an instant with no help from people, places, times or events.

All your energy will be available to use and manifest the new car which you so desire. Consciousness works in this way and you are learning to increase your vibration and frequency. By letting go of past events that caused trauma and emotional scarring to the mental, emotional and physical bodies, you are freeing up your body from blocked energy and increasing your awareness and consciousness. You are freeing your mind from thoughts that keep you trapped in the past or future.

The day will come when nothing will resemble the present, and that, too, will be good. Liberate yourself from past events and experiences that are holding you back and start to be present in the moment. The quantum field is always present in the now. The past is in the human mind as this is the only place where it can exist, nowhere on the planet does the past exist – it cannot, it's the past.

Our minds keep the past alive in our memory. We need to let go of the thinking mind and our need to relive the past. If we don't we will consciously create the future from our past and hence we will be stuck in our past. Do you understand what I am saying? The past keeps you trapped in a world that does not exist and will never exist again. You, however, give life to the past by bringing it into the now and that reaffirms the events and experiences of the past.

This is an absolute crucial teaching that the world needs to understand: never should you hold onto the past as it keeps your energy locked and trapped in the past moment. How can you then move forward? You can only move forward once you stop thinking about the past, enabling yourself to create more in the now.

Video cameras and photos are a snapshot of the past and too often we want to relive a specific moment in time. Let it go, it does not serve you and your mind will keep on referencing the moment as long as you keep the past alive in the mind. Look at the past, learn from the past, and move forward in life always in the now.

Once you do, your every moment in life will be more glorious and happy. You will have learnt a valuable lesson that by bringing the past to life only reaffirms the past in the now. Stop holding on, break up with the past and never go back. It's impossible to recreate an event in order to have the same experience; no event is ever the same. The feelings and emotions that the now hold are vastly more joyous and exhilarating. When you stay in the past, you are being trapped in an old movie which keeps on playing over and over.

When energy is trapped at a specific moment in time, your emotions and feelings are trapped in that moment. The same goes for the bad experience which life might have dished out to you. Emotions and feelings might be locked at a point in time where you experienced anger, sadness or loss which needs to be released. Only until you surrender and accept that the past experience was there to help you grow, will you find peace.

Feelings of the past have no power in the now, they only gain power when you reference these old feelings or emotions and bring them into the now. We have the potential to create and recreate anything in the quantum field of possibilities by bringing the past into the now.

Do you understand this very important life lesson? Stop looking back and move forward in life, release the old emotions of the past and move forward by creating new experiences. Pursue new and exciting ideas of what you would love to experience and accomplish. Stop and free your energy from the ties that bind your mind to the past.

One day the world will understand the real value of this teaching and lesson. On that day the collective consciousness of the world will be so evolved and know that God *Is*, meaning forever in the now.

Be happy, laugh and play more, let go of all past regrets. You are God and have the ability to move yourself into the present whenever you so desire. Do you desire the past? As the past will then be your present. You are the master of your mind and have full domain over every thought which enters. Surrender your old thinking habits which keep you locked in the past or future and start to live in the now with your full presence of being.

Exercise 10 – Emotional energy releasing

Now it's time to do some intense emotional energy releasing work. Focus on an emotion or emotions that are most prevalent and consuming of your human mind at this time. Focus on an event or situation that left you feeling either depressed, sad, angered, irritated, enraged, unhappy or bitter. Make sure you have ample time, as you may need an hour or more to complete this exercise.

Next, sit quietly and ask the following three questions to yourself, allowing for some time after each question so that the answers may come to you.

- Why am I feeling this way?
- How was I responsible for attracting the event or situation into my life?
- What is the lesson or lessons I need to learn in order for me to move forward?

The answers to these questions are inside you. Time is of no essence, so take your time, no need to rush through the process. Speak to your God and have the messages of intuitive thought be your guide to the answers. Write all answers down on paper.

After the answers to the above three questions have become clear to you, I want you to find a safe space where you can vent and not be disturbed. I want you to go for a walk in nature, along the seashore, sit quietly or put on your boxing gloves;

whilst contemplating the answer to question one, 'why am I feeling this way?' While you are contemplating the question, I want you to go into feeling the emotion or emotions that have come up, whether depressed, sad, angry, enraged, irritated, unhappy or bitter.

Force and push yourself to go into feeling the emotion or emotions! Let the feeling find you; shouting and screaming at the top of your lungs or hitting a punching bag, crying and weeping from utter depression and sadness, by being totally enraged with anger at the event or situation. Do not stop until you have released all the blocked negative energy from emotions associated with the event or situation from your body. You might go from anger, to depression and sadness and that's wonderful, as you are going through the stages of grief and healing. You might even need to repeat this step more than once in order to release all the blocked energy and emotions.

These emotions carry negative energy connected to them, which we want to release from your body's cellular structure. All negative emotions keep a part of your energy trapped in the past at a point in time where you had a so-called, 'bad' experience of trauma or pain. Your body's cellular structure locks in the negative energy from the event or situation, with the assistance from your human mind's perception. This could result and be the cause for cancer or other bodily diseases.

From childhood we are never truly shown and taught how to deal with our so-called, 'bad' emotional experiences and wounds. As men, we are not allowed to cry, and as women, we are said to be too emotional and need to toughen up. You may have gone through many perceived 'bad' experiences, causing emotional and energetic blockages along the journey of life as you never dealt with the trauma of the issue then and there.

Forgive yourself, the other person or persons, the event or situation and forget any existence thereof in any form or matter. Never look back to the past! Your goal should be to work your way back, like peeling the layers of the onion, in order to release and let go of each of your so-called 'bad' experiences, and move forward. With stripping the layers, you are freeing yourself from the entrapments of your human mind's perception, and increasing your frequency and vibration by enhancing your invisible light body[44]; making way for more happiness, joy and love to enter your life.

Question two, 'how was I responsible for attracting the event or situation into my life?' What are the answers that you received from your God? As mentioned earlier, we attract events or situations into our life by way of our thinking, words and actions, or past life Karma that someday has to be released. See the event or situation as a string of energy being pulled, holding your human mind enslaved to an old way of thinking.

Follow the same process as you did for question one, but this time accept that you had a part to play in creating the event or situation. Forgive yourself for not seeing things as just an experience, by not classifying it as either 'good or bad'. Free yourself and others of all judgments, blame and guilt associated with the event or situation and set your human mind free.

Lastly, what is the lesson or lessons I ought to learn in order for me to move forward?' All life lessons ultimately lead to a greater love for self and love for others!

In truth there is actually nothing to forgive as the past does not exist in the Mind of God.

---

[44] Also known as your ethereal or spiritual body.

A word of caution, please seek professional support if you have experienced severe mental, emotional and physical trauma, as you may need some ongoing support to release the blocked negative emotions and energy.

YOUR MIND HAS THE POWER
TO CREATE A MAGICAL NOW

YOU SHOULD NEVER STOP DREAMING as your dreams may one day become a reality. The quantum field always listens to your thoughts and creates for you that which you desire. With our minds we create our future, and we should focus on what it is we would like to attract into our lives. We should hold the vision of the object or experience clearly in our mind's eye, but with no emotional and time connection.

In undertaking the above you are designing your future, but leave room for change and redesign. Don't get so stuck on dreaming about the future that you forget to live in the now. You should hold the dream clear and have your mind find a way to make your dream a reality. Your God will do the rest by using your consciousness and energy out of the quantum field to manifest your desire into your physical reality. Listen and then take action to create and manifest your reality.

Are you following me or do you need a grander explanation? God lives only in the now and the now is all God knows; all potentials and possibilities exist simultaneously in this very moment, and you have free choice which one to explore and live. There is a potential for every dream you have ever dreamt to be manifested right this very moment. For this very reason whatever you are doing right now was a dream which you dreamt and wanted to experience.

I trust you are following my explanation, which actually implies that you are always at the right place and time. Never are you not where you wanted to be even in sorrow, grief, anger, fear, loss, death, love, peace, joy, happiness, success, etc; you are always where you dreamt you wanted to be. Never are you anywhere else but present in the moment of now. For those of you having trouble grasping the above concept, I suggest that you re-read the last three sections starting with 'Live to experience the wonder of life's infinite possibilities', whilst you contemplate on this concept, until you fully understand and make it your own.

YOU ARE A MOVIE STAR IN THE QUANTUM FIELD

THE EARTH HAS AN ELECTROMAGNETIC grid that keeps us all connected and intertwined with each other in the quantum field. See the earth as one giant movie screen, with you as an actor playing a role in a movie. You have free choice to alter the role or modify the scenes you are appearing in. See yourself as the lead actor of this movie being played and everybody else as your supporting and co-actors.

You have free rein to create whatever movie your heart desires, your mental projection bringing the manifestation of this movie to life. Nobody in this movie can tell you where you should go or what you should be doing; this is entirely up to you. At the same time you are the actor, writer and director of this movie. You have free will to change the screen play at any time you so desire. All you need to do is place a new picture of what you want to experience in your mind's eye. In doing so you are placing the new image into your quantum field.

You need to believe that this new role and picture is already in motion. When you follow this principle the universe and quantum field will deliver the experience to you. You do not have to know how, all you need to do is ask with pure intent for assistance and know the new role and picture has already been gifted to you by the grace of your God.

The quantum system is designed for each person to play the role destined and designed for them by them. There is no need for competition as each person is uniquely suited for their role and is the only person able to play their role. We are all actors and co-actors in each other's movies, with varying degrees of relatedness due to the interconnectedness of the planet. No person can view your movie through their eyes; you are the only person fit for your role.

The earth has over 7 billion movie stars with a dynamic and ever-changing script being played out by each of the stars. You are creating your world within the greater world. Actually, what you are doing is shifting your energy around according to your beliefs, views, patterns and role being portrayed. You have full control over your attitude, beliefs, values and views; and in the end, over your world. The system is designed for each human to create and live their dreams, by making their own movie come to life.

You have a variety of relationships in your movie, each influencing the roles being played by those around you or that you come in contact with. Having mentioned the above, you, however, have no influence over a co-actor's attitude, beliefs or views. They decide for themselves with their own freewill and choice how they want to act or feel in their movie and reality. You cannot make someone feel loved or sad if they do not choose to.

Each actor has a unique agenda creating their little world within the bigger world, their reality within a greater reality. The actions and reactions of each actor influence the interconnectedness of the whole. There are those actors, who have similar dreams, and these actors, to an extent, create movies and worlds together; but nobody can enter the inner sanctum of your dream and movie.

With each step you are weaving the tapestry of your life and having an effect on the whole. You are the law in your movie and world, you define your truth!

THE TRANSFORMATION OF OLD ENERGY TO CREATE HEAVEN ON EARTH

THE FUTURE IS ALWAYS HAPPENING in the now as the future does not exist separately; God is everywhere, always in the now. We have lived in survival mode for the past few millennia and it's time for us to take back our power and become Gods living in the present with no thought of the past and continuously making known the unknown.

We have been living in a three dimensional world - no, actually, a four dimensional world, when you include time. We are plagued by our past and scared to live in the now, forever planning our future with no room for change towards our goals. The goal is far more magnificent than we can even begin to imagine once we start to listen to our intuition. We then surrender the mind's need for understanding and reasoning.

The four dimensional system was designed for human survival, with our intellectual mind geared to analyze, rationalize and use logic up to this point in order to survive. We are moving into a new era of physical living, a closer connection to the spiritual world where basic human logic does not apply; where we walk with faith, an internal knowingness that guides each individual to their highest excelsior as we create heaven on earth.

To be a quantum warrior you need to surrender to the observer self and start to live a life being constantly focused in the present moment. We have no idea where we will be in a year or even the next day, so surrender and let your God take over and make your every move. We are entering higher dimensions and planes of existence as we let go of the human mind and follow the quantum Mind of God. We are activating the Higher Self and building the bridge of understanding very slowly.

Over-thinking corrupts the present moment, and these thoughts need to be eradicated from our mind. Only one thought can occupy our mind at any time, and that thought can either fester like a disease growing, expanding and causing suffering, or can create peace and harmony for the individual. Suffering only exists because of the two worlds which do not exist, the past and future. If you are truly fully in the now there is no suffering, as all your needs are always met in the moment.

Once you let go of the thinking human mind all suffering ceases to exist, making way for states of peace, bliss, joy and happiness to enter your being. Hence the saying, 'live each moment like there is no tomorrow'. There is no need to suffer, as you do not have a past, and the future does not exist. Can you for sure know where you are going to be in a year's time? No! So then, stop living there, and stay in the now.

Consciousness has no association with the human intellectual mind, and thus the brightest people on the planet might not have the highest consciousness. The intellect uses reason and logic, whereas consciousness is in every respect intertwined with your level of caring, compassion, love, intuition and awareness. You can call consciousness your 'sixth sense', with more people around the world tuning into their own unique frequency. This is the next step in our evolution: developing aspects of intuitive thought by trusting life and the path we are walking.

The intellectual and human thinking mind is one and the same, and cannot take you to higher planes of existence. Your sixth sense and observer self is your quantum part and can elevate your being into new paradigms and planes of reality. As you raise your energy and consciousness, so will you grow in your understanding of reality and the truth about your God – ever-present and quantumly connected. The quantum field in your mind ties and connects all of your neighbours and the whole world, *the oneness principle.*

YOU ARE LIVING ALL YOUR LIVES PAST, PRESENT AND FUTURE NOW

DID YOU KNOW THAT YOUR past, present and future lives are all being lived in the now? Yes, this is true; as we only have the now. This concept is a difficult one for the human mind to comprehend, as our logical mind does not allow for this understanding. How can it be anything other than the now? We have discussed 'the now' at length, and thus you should be starting to understand that the now is all there is. Ponder on this for a while whilst you connect to your greater part that knows; your spirit and God.

Life after life is being lived in the now as God exists only in the now. God only resides in the present. God has no past and has no future, God just *Is*. Do you understand? If not, let me explain a little further and hopefully you will be able to make sense of this concept in some way. You have lived forever and will live forever – maybe not in the physical but in spirit. Your spirit never dies, it just transforms into higher dimensions of energy and light upon your death. You cross the veil back into the spirit world, joining up with all the other parts of you in God. Like a drop being part of the ocean, so are you part of God's spectacular tapestry.

Take out a pen and paper and write the word 'love'. Once you have finished writing the word, the act becomes part of your past. You cannot ever get back these few seconds; they are gone for all eternity. So why do we cling onto the past? We know the past; it's comfortable and safe and therefore we want to keep it alive. What would happen if we took time and space out of our reality? Our reality would cease to exist and all would merge into one. The universe would retract back into nothingness.

The same principle applies with all lives being lived in the now; if you were to take time out of the equation we would be everything and all things known. However, due to the dimension of time, we are able to experience the now continuously and are creating the future always in the now.

We have been blinded by the 'fact' that we have a past or a future. Yet these elements do not exist and are merely an illusion created for the sake of experience. Thus, time after time, we come back to earth with a new body in order to elevate our light spectrum and catapult ourselves into becoming whole, a 'God-man' realized. Each time we enter with a new body it is the same time as now, each and all experiences we are having are taking place in this very moment, this split second.

Time does not exist for God and was created solely for the purpose of the soul to journey through life and all its illusions. There are many who are unaware of this principle, and as we grow in consciousness so do we grow in awareness, as the two are inseparable. With each shift in awareness there is more compassion, love and joy that fill our hearts. We realize that nobody can break our heart as our heart can never be broken - another of the mind's great illusions.

KNOWLEDGE AND WISDOM BRINGS PEACE THROUGH UNDERSTANDING

WHEN YOU START TO LIVE *the oneness principle*, you start to see the world as a beautiful movie picture in which you are acting and watching at the same time as each second of life unfolds. You have full power over your actions, emotions and feelings during each stage of the movie. You are only responsible for your actions, not the actions of others. You live like you have no tomorrow, embracing and valuing each second for the lessons and gifts they hold.

You stop taking life too seriously and learn to have fun, relax and play more. You find more enjoyment in the quantum system as you now understand it is all a big game, designed and created by you and all the other souls, to take pleasure in and love. You surrender to the process of life and become a traveller being guided by your God along all life's enchanting moments. You cherish each second as you have gained new knowledge which lead to new wisdom in that there might not be a next moment.

You start to see each person as family and not strangers, prisoners or beggars. You stop judging them and allow them to be who they want to be. You understand that you are here to be you and nobody else. You realize that you are far greater than your physical body, that you are eternal and can never die. You release the worries of the world and start to grasp that infinite possibilities are available to you.

Collectively we have the power to change and correct the injustices of the past, living a life in harmony like never before experienced on this planet. The quantum field is an ever-changing energy field, dissolving and reappearing a few times each second, too fast for the naked eye to see. For that reason, we do not just live each lifetime – past, present or future – in the now; we live each second in the now as that is the only moment there is in God.

Our Higher Self is the driver, and when we hold a thought and picture in our frontal lobes we start to create from this point, holding the image clear with no interference as though it is already an existing reality. Why do you think so many sports men and woman play the game or see their race in their mind's eye before the actual game? They are visualizing, projecting and constructing mental images to generate a positive outcome for themselves.

This is how the Masters we all love so much were able to disappear and reappear within a split second. Their whole auric or energy field is free to manifest at will bread, fish, wine and more from the quantum field. They know the laws of science and spirit and studied both. What a glorious and superb puzzle we are navigating. Can you begin to imagine the magnitude, the phenomenon? If you can't, best you start to contemplate the enormity and value of each second you're alive and breathing.

CATASTROPHIC EVENTS AFFECT THE COLLECTIVE CONSCIOUSNESS OF EARTH

THIS BRINGS ME TO MY second last topic: that of global catastrophic and disastrous events. These events have a direct effect on the collective consciousness of the world. Why do I say this? I say this as we are all one which you now know, and thus have a direct and indirect impact on the whole planet. The terror of September 11 or '911' as referred to by people; the tragedy of Haiti and other global disasters had a direct influence on the planet and consciousness of the whole.

With each tragic event, we experience and feel an emotion being released, called 'compassion'. Compassion is the result of empathy being displayed for victims. Deep feelings of love and compassion were felt by many during these times as their hearts were extended to the victims, sufferers and families of these tragic events. There was a spike in the quantum field and the collective consciousness of the whole, due to an increase of love and compassion.[45] This brought forth a greater sense for the value of human life and unity in these countries.

With every disaster, we shift in consciousness and awareness; even world wars have a profound influence on those who were caught up in the terrifying ordeal. They know the feeling of

---

[45] See info on Global Consciousness Project: http://en.wikipedia.org/wiki/Global_Consciousness_Project

being unsafe, scared, not having enough food to eat, and the utter despair associated with war. Their consciousness and soul has full account of these horrifying and awful acts. They do not want to relive these times ever again as the anguish, torment and pain was extremely hard to bear. I know this. I experienced it.

They want peace, they want freedom, they want to live and enjoy life the way we were meant to. Every tragedy has a silver lining and increases the awareness of those involved; even the ones who are watching are affected by these events. Tragic events have the capability to open the hearts of millions, as empathy is the ability to put yourself in another person's shoes and feel their pain and hurt.

This is what 911 and Haiti did for me. I was in the USA when the events of 911 transpired. I had been visiting friends in LA, about to fly to New York. I had just boarded the plane which was about to take-off and in the end, never did. A ground stop was declared and the whole USA and world was up in arms. This had to happen to make people see what unity and oneness is all about. What the words 'freedom' and 'liberty' truly mean, not just idle words spoken in vein.

This event set in motion one of the biggest acts of compassion the world has ever seen. The event increased the consciousness of the collective like never before on this planet. Tragedy is a catalyst for transformation; retaliation is a weak person's way to cope with wounds of the past.

Haiti was another disaster, with a gigantic earthquake striking and devastating the country, causing the loss of so many lives. I felt this to the core of my being. I recall feeling extremely sad and depressed on this particular day, not truly understanding the main cause of my sadness. Only after a friend called and told me about the magnitude and scale of the event did I start to recognize why I felt so sad. We are all connected and in more ways than you might realize.

Chile experienced a similar display of compassion with the disaster where a group of miners were trapped underground for almost 70 days. The whole country showed strong empathy for the trapped workers and their grief-stricken families. All prayed endlessly for the miners' rescue and safe passage home. The Chilean people pulled together as one nation during this tragic event and displayed true compassionate action.

These are but a few of the events over a time span of a mere two decades that have changed our planet forever. Energy and consciousness shifts slowly, as the choice is always up to the individual or individuals involved. These are sad and tragic stories, but they helped the earth shift and show more compassion for our fellow human beings. Nothing goes unnoticed by your God and even in these difficult and hard times your spirit and God is always with you.

All those who endured the adversity and hardship of these events had their God with them, in the form of the ever-present observer self. There is never any judgment from your Higher Self and it knows of the potential that exists whereby you might be passing over to the other side of the veil. I believe, that at the point of crossing over, we may choose our welcome home party to be present, and thus are mostly greeted by already passed-on loved ones as they wait and assist with your safe passage back to the light.

I want you to once again see the earth as one gigantic movie, with you and the entire human race as the actors, playing out the infinite number of potentials by making known the unknown. There is no script - the script is being written and played at the same time, each second in the now. You dream your dream and play your part to the best you know how. Have faith in the process and know life may bring you a few unexpected events along the journey.

JOSHUA BEN JOSEPH - JESUS

BEFORE I CLOSE, I WANT to share my view and truth around the death of one of the most loved beings to have ever walked our planet, Joshua Ben Joseph known to most as Jesus. Jesus is a Master Prophet, and had perfected his mastery in the East before returning to the Middle East where he gave numerous public lectures and speeches about love and the power that love holds.

To this day, history shows that he single-handedly changed the course and direction of our entire planet. His prophecy is ageless and will never die, as truth cannot die. He walked with dignity, grace and poise; a humble and loving man who touched the heart of each person he met. He had integrated the trinity of the One: God the Father, God the Son and the Holy Spirit.

He was destined to be crucified, he knew his fate, and such is mentioned in the Bible.[46] The point I want to make is that his God wanted to experience death and transcend the claws thereof. His Higher Self wanted him to die, not to save the world from 'sin and evil' but to show to all people what

---

[46] New American Standard Bible, New Testament in the book of Matthew 26:39 - 'And He went a little beyond them, and fell on His face and prayed, saying, 'My Father, if it is possible, let this cup pass from Me; yet not as I will, but as You will'.' I would however suggest that you read the chapter 26 in its entirety.

is available for them on the planet. We all have the ability to liberate ourselves from the clutches of death.

Do not fear death, as it can be overcome, but only once you meld and become one with your Higher Self, the eternal observer self. Jesus had merged with his Higher Self and followed the path he was destined to. One day all will know and recognize that within each one of us lies a 'Christ' just waiting to be given free rein to discover and explore the world and entire universe.

Nothing is impossible – if you can think it, it's possible. Why do you think so many movies about superheroes, time travel and levitation are being made? More of these old powers will be given back to us the more energy we shift and grow in consciousness. The allowance for these gifts in life comes from dedication, hard work and unconditional love, by becoming one with your Higher Self. These aren't mere fallacies, they are real, and we are being watched by the whole of creation from above, below, in and around.

Exercise 11 – Facing your fears

As we journey through life we will have to face many fears, looking them straight in the eyes, and many times over. Fear is not real; it is the absence of love. Fear is the ultimate illusion created by the human mind in order to trap our mind in the past or in the future, by separating you from God's love. Danger is real, but fear is not. In the present moment fear cannot and does not exist.

Fear is made real by thinking and analyzing the 'what ifs' in life. What if that happened to me? As we walk through life and grow in our consciousness we will be faced with numerous fears; the fear of not having enough food to eat, warmth or shelter, fear of death, fear of certain animals, insects or reptiles, fear of public speaking, fear of water and swimming in the sea, fear of heights or enclosed spaces, fear of riding a bicycle, the fear of being alone, fear of losing or failure – hence no participation, fear of being rejected – hence no intimacy, fear of being cheated on – hence the fear of relationships, fear of missing out, fear of duality and letting go thereof. Even to the point of having to overcome the fear of success and being more successful than ever before. However, the biggest fear you will have to face is the fear of the unknown and to trust the process of life.

What do you fear in life? Make a comprehensive list of all the fears that your mind has created and made so real. One by one, you want to look at each fear. Face each one, by starting with the easy ones. For example, if you fear public speaking start practicing speaking in front of people, or enrol in a public speaking course or Toastmasters[47] to assist you. Allow for time as this is a slow process and it may take time to release just one. With each fear that you overcome, there is a death to a section of your human mind, ego and personality; and a shift in energy leading to more freedom.

FEAR = False Events Appearing Real!

---

[47] See Toastmasters on: www.toastmasters.org/

EPILOGUE

WE ARE BEING PROTECTED BY a higher power to move the earth into a new paradigm of existence and enjoy a more fruitful life, with greater love and compassion for all we meet and connect with. All life is sacred and nothing goes unnoticed by the eternal God-Mind and your Higher Self. You are divinely protected and supported by your Higher Self and can never *not* be part of the whole. Always give thanks for another day and live each moment as though it is your last with full passion and commitment to your God.

Never allow for anyone to tell you how to react or how to feel. Each person is special and forms a part of the whole. We have all come to earth to navigate and explore this magical puzzle. God lives through you, as you, and you have the ability to connect to your Higher Self at any time you so wish. Live like there's no tomorrow, and know your Higher Self is there to guide you – all answers are a mere question away.

Open your heart and let it be filled with the joy and love of your God. Give of yourself and be at peace with your every choice and decision. There is no need to regret anything in life, as you were guided to that point and choice. So what if it was not the best choice? Hopefully the next time you will do better as you would have learnt from your mistakes. There is no need to ever judge yourself; lovingly accept who you are.

Love yourself first and above all, and love your neighbour and all with the same passion and dedication. Never allow for anyone to guide you; ask your God for guidance. The truth for each person is situated within their heart and your heart is also the place where the answers to all your questions lie. Allow for time and listen to the answers you receive. Remember who you are and connect every day with that higher intelligence, the part of you that is one with everything through the Mind of God.

Love is all there is and your desire should be fully focused on being loving in each moment. Even in times where you have to say no to people and to actions that compromise your integrity, do it with respect and honour. Allow for mistakes and avoid those that want to pull you down. Be the example to all others and show them the way by being sincere and humble.

Never stop loving, feel the Creator's love deep within your heart and surrender the hurt of the past to God. Remember, the past does not exist and all there is, is the eternal now. Be at peace with all your actions and give with all your heart. Rejoice in life by enjoying all its pleasures, but remember to do unto others that which you want done unto you. Such is the law of Karma, the law of cause and effect, 'that as you sow you shall reap'.

Your heart cannot be broken; you are the director and conductor of what you allow by your thinking. The mind plays tricks and needs to be kept at bay and we should not allow for any negativity to enter. You are far more than the human mind and what you appear to be; all the world's power and strength rest inside you. All you need to do is go within, to the core of your being, to your heart, and unleash this wisdom into the world for all to bear witness.

Life is there to support your every effort; have patience with each step along the journey. Take time to relax and gather new energy as the journey is meant to be one of excitement and splendour. The quantum system is filled with endless and infinite possibilities to be explored and experienced. You are ageless, you are immortal, you are eternal, and you are divine with no beginning and no end.

How does the above sound to you? Can you feel it in your body? I can, and I know that soon one day, within a split second, the magnitude of these words will sink into the core of my being. I long for that day when all disease and lack will finally wither away and bring rise to a new 'Christ' in me and you. Until the dawn of that day I will be focused in the present and live each second like a warrior of light, unfaltering to the end.

Can you comprehend the idea that God knows every hair on your body? If you can, ask yourself the next question: 'how much more does this great and mysterious presence know about who I am?' There is so much more to make known, you have but touched a speckle in the sky. Never think you know everything and seize each moment to learn something new.

You might say, 'this is all beautiful and great, but how do I meld with my Higher Self?' The journey for each person is different, and with that the experiences each person has asked to have are different upon entering the physical plane of existence. With that said, never look at another and yearn for the same; rather, make your own path by following your heart.

There are as many ways to enlightenment or up the mountain as there are drops in the ocean. What works for me may not work for you. Find your niche and persist with your whole being, and every time you feel stuck, change your path and try something new. A great variety of meditations and spiritual disciplines are available for you to use along your journey.

Go to lectures and participate in courses that allow you to shift your perspective and view of life. Learn from many teachers and masters, but regard life as your greatest teacher. Never feel the need to prove your knowledge and wisdom to anybody. Find your truth and live your truth each moment.

Know that along the way you will be required to conquer many obstacles and barriers. Surrender your need to be right, and allow for the magic find you. Create a foundation that works for you, and follow the signs which are gifted to you by your God. Let intuition and synchronicity guide your every step to infinity.

Your soul is on a maiden voyage of discovery, reaching planes and dimensions never seen before. Your soul wants to soar above previously self-imposed limits by making known the unknown. Love your every footstep and 'but seek first His kingdom and His righteousness, and all these things will be added to you,' as said by Jesus in the Bible.[48]

Within the sanctum of your heart lies the truth you need to uncover. Love yourself, love all people, animals, plants, trees, insects. Love all life with sincere care and compassion.

In writing this book I know that God has no structure and cannot be placed in a box. God has no box; God is fully quantum and completely unstructured and formless, and does not make human logical sense. The beginning is the end and the end is the beginning. God is ageless and timeless, forever existing in the now.

God just Is.

---

[48] New American Standard Bible, New Testament in the book of Matthew 6:33 and for a cross reference see Luke 12:31 - 'But seek His kingdom, and these things will be added to you.'

Exercise 12 – Write a poem or song

Have some fun and play by exploring and taking some time to focus on writing a poem or song from your heart. I want you to feel it in the core of your being and into life. You can write about anything as long as you are expressing your love. There are no wrongs or rights, this is a personal adventure of going within and letting the magic and inspiration of divine love find you. One and all can do this exercise. The act may gift and leave you with an astounding sense of awe and accomplishment. As an example I would like to share a deeply personal poem that I wrote at the age of 15.

Poem – To my dream girl

I had her for a while
But not for a long time
I made the mistake to leave her
I thought I was too good for her

Now I'm loving her more than ever
More than she'll ever know
The girl that I've known forever
And the girl I want to be with from now

I wish I knew how to get her
So that we could be together
But I've got no courage to face her
She has had a few boyfriends, since I had left her

Now I'm loving her more than ever
More than she's ever know
The girl that I've known forever
And the girl I want to be with from now

When will she see the love that I have for her
The love that's bubbling in my heart is for her
She's broken my heart again
She got a new guy

But I'm still loving her more than ever
More than she'll ever know
The girl that I've known forever
And the girl that I want to be with from now

She has been dating him for a while
I wish that I could be with her all that time
But it's not to be
She is loving him and not me.

My love is stronger than ever
More than she'll ever know
The girl that I've known forever
And the girl I want to be with from now

It's been a few months now
They have had a bit of trouble now
She's broken up with him
Now I'll wait and see what happens

I wish I knew how to tell her
That I love her
The girl I've known forever
And the girl I want to be with forever

AUTHOR'S NOTES

IF YOU HAVE ENJOYED *'The Magic of Quantum Living'*, I highly recommend the following books, audios and DVD's.

'The Shack' by William Young
'Living A Course in Miracles' by Jon Mundy
'The Four Agreements' and *'Mastery of Love'* by Don Miguel Ruiz
'Conversations with God' – Book one, two and three by Neale Donald Walsch
'The Power of Now' and *'A New Earth'* by Eckhart Tolle
'Journey of Souls' by Michael Newton
'Power vs. Force' by David R Hawkins
'The Seven Spiritual Laws' by Deepak Chopra

'Kryon Channelling' (Free audio) by Lee Carroll – www.kryon.com
'The Secret' (DVD) by Rhonde Byrne – www.thesecret.tv
'You Can Heal Your Life' – The movie (DVD) by Louise Hay – www.hayhouse.com
'The Divine Matrix' (DVD's) by Gregg Braden – www.greggbraden.com

These are just some of the sources that I have used over the past few years. I do, however, recommend and suggest if you are keen on implementing the knowledge from these resources that you attend workshops, lectures and talks as shifting personal awareness and consciousness is amplified in a collective group.

Visit: www.theonenessprinciple.co.za if you would like to take this knowledge further.